Healing Humanity
Time, Touch & Talk

Richard Cohen, M.A.

TTT Press
Bowie, Maryland

TTT Press
P.O. Box 2315
Bowie, MD 20718
Tel. (301) 805-5155
Fax (301) 805-0182
Email: TTT@TimeTouchandTalk.com
Web: www.TimeTouchandTalk.com

© Richard Cohen, M.A., 2019

All rights reserved. No part of this book may be reproduced or translated in any form without permission from the publisher. No part of this book may be reproduced, stored in or introduced into a retrieval system, or transmitted, in any form or by any means (electronic, mechanical, photocopying, recording, or otherwise) without the prior written permission of the publisher.

This publication is designed to provide accurate and authoritative information in regard to the subject matter covered. It is sold with the understanding that the publisher is not engaged in rendering legal, counseling, medical, or therapeutic services. If legal, medical, therapeutic or other expert assistance is required, the services of a competent professional person should be sought.

Most names have been changed to protect the confidentiality of those who willingly shared their stories for the benefit of others.

Cover design: Roland Owusu-Tabi / www.rolgh.com
Book layout design: Lisa DeSpain / www.book2bestseller.com
All photos: www.iStockphoto.com
All charts, drawings, and diagrams: www.Fiverr.com
ISBN 978-1-7338469-6-7
Printed in the United States of America

Library of Congress Control Number: 2019904078

Cohen, Richard, 1952, October 15
Healing Humanity: Time, Touch, and Talk
ISBN 978-1-7338469-0-5
1. Self-help
2. Psychology
3. Sexuality

Dedication

I dedicate this book to God. You gave me life. You saved my life over and over again.

I dedicate this book to my faithful and loving wife Jae Sook, and our three amazing adult children—Jarish, Jessica, and Alfred.

I dedicate this book to these inspiring and incredible Godly men and women without whom this book would never have been published: Pastor John & Trina Jenkins, Bishop Alfred & Susie Owens, Pastor Keith & Vicki Battle, and Pastor Ron & Brenda Crawford.

A special thanks to my dear friends Phillip Schanker and Mary Hamm for your invaluable assistance in editing the manuscript multiple times. You both went above and beyond. I can't thank you enough. Additional thanks to my other proof readers: Lily Oliveri, Kari Clewett, Xan Woolsey, ShehabEldeen Elhawary, Pilar Schanker, Caleb Brundidge, Wenda Fry, and Jae Sook Cohen.

I dedicate this book to you, the reader. Let us work hand-in-hand and heart-to-heart to heal the world through healthy Time, Touch & Talk.

Contents

Introduction 7
Prologue 15
Time, Touch & Talk Outline 18
TIME 21
    Self-Healing 24
    Family Healing 99
    Community Healing 116
TOUCH 119
    Self-Healing 126
    Family Healing 193
    Community Healing 210
TALK 221
    Self-Healing 223
    Family Healing 237
    Community Healing 254
Conclusion: Final Touch! 261
References for Further Healing 275
Family Healing Sessions 277
About the Author 279
Photo of Author in Montserrat Monastery 281

Introduction*

> "It is easier to build strong children than to repair broken men." —Frederick Douglass

Time, Touch & Talk, or TTT, is the missing link to help you fulfill your basic needs for belonging, bonding, and connection, and to help you become the person you are truly meant to be.

When I told one of my friends I was writing a book about healing the world through healthy touch he said, "Richard, people don't have a clue that they need healthy touch!"

To which I replied, "True. And that's what I hope to show them—that this is a core truth that runs through the veins of every child, adolescent, and adult upon the earth."

Robert Bly has written, "Our gift comes through the wound." And to begin with, I'll share just a few simple facts about my own wounds: When I was five years old, my NFL Hall of Fame Uncle turned me into his sex partner for almost one year—teaching me how to please him, while he used my body for his pleasure.

My father, Samuel Cohen, was a World War II veteran, whose Marine platoon helped put up the flag at Iwo Jima. After seeing his comrades murdered left and right, he came home and bombarded us with his anger and rage almost every day of my childhood. I felt as if I grew up in war. In those days, there was little understanding about Post-Traumatic Stress Disorder (PTSD).

My brother was almost five years my senior. Neal was the chief recipient of my father's hostility. But he then projected his anger and pain onto me, physically beating me throughout our childhood. I fought back, but the size difference always left me a loser.

My older sister, Lyd, was the apple of my father's eye and could do no wrong. My mother was horrified by my father's rage and didn't know where to hide. Since I was the youngest, mom held me while she cried out the pain of her seemingly hopeless existence. I felt her agony, but didn't know what to do—take care of her pain, or deal with the pain I felt? She was never a safe person for me.

Growing up in an upper-middle class Jewish family outside of Philadelphia in the 1950s, our family must have looked like the Ozzie and Harriet show from the outside. However, behind closed doors it felt like war.

I had three safe places: 1) Dancing under the street lamps when everyone was asleep, 2) Running naked in the rain at nighttime in an open field behind our home, and 3) Attending a gospel church many Sunday mornings with our housekeeper Ophelia—a woman who felt more like a mother to me than my own Mom.

Today my wife and I attend at least two churches—Catholic Mass at our local parish, and an African-American church (more about this later). While attending Boston University, I danced with an African-American company created by a former Alvin Ailey dancer. I was the only white man in a black company! Everyone would sit around Harvard square after rehearsals bemoaning racial bigotry in the 60s and 70s. I could understand their pain, and yet a part of me was screaming inside, "But you don't know what it's like growing up in a war zone on 15 Greenhill Lane in

Philadelphia and experiencing homosexual feelings in a straight family and community."

While attending Boston University in the 70s, I had a male partner for three years. It was through him that I came to believe in Christ. This was yet another departure from the norm of the Cohen Jewish family and community. I was both Bar Mitzvahed and confirmed in our local synagogue. Yet, still, in my heart, I cherished a dream of marrying a woman and having children. It was not religion, society, my parents, or social pressure that initiated this concept in my soul. It was a dream that was planted deep in my heart from childhood. And having sexual feelings for men was an obstacle to achieving my goal.

Therapy, my faith, and the love of several extraordinary men and women helped me resolve my unwanted same-sex attractions. I reconciled with my parents, grieved the pain of sexual abuse, and learned to receive real love from others. Today I have been married to my beautiful wife Jae Sook since 1980, and we have three amazing adult children. Dreams do come true!

I've been a psychotherapist since 1989, and have helped thousands of individuals, couples, and families throughout the world. I have also trained over 6,000 psychotherapists, psychiatrists, counselors, coaches, clergy, and ministry leaders.

So why is a guy who had homosexual partners and is now married to a woman with three adult-children writing a book about *Healing Humanity: Time, Touch & Talk*? Simply put, I am deeply aware of the damaging effects of touch deprivation, and the misuse of touch and its many ramifications. These issues relating to touch affect the lives of millions of men and women worldwide, for whom sex has become a substitute for genuine love and affection.

I clearly see how the world could be revolutionized through healthy parent-child bonding, increased healthy touch between family members, friends, co-workers, and everyone in our lives. Research shows that healthy touch increases our overall sense of wellbeing, reduces stress, promotes happiness, improves health, increases work productivity, and creates a brighter future (Retrieved from: https://www.khca.org/files/2015/10/8-Reasons-Why-We-Need-Human-Touch-More-Than-Ever.pdf).

In the pages that follow, you will read my "manifesto" to revolutionize the world through healthy Time, Touch & Talk, or TTT. On January 8, 1997, God gave me the concept for this book, and eventually a worldwide project. It has been percolating in my mind, heart, body, and spirit since that day.

Today is the perfect time for its release. We are bombarded with the outing of Hollywood moguls, political giants, business tycoons, and religious leaders for sexually abusing and misusing men, women, adolescents, and children. Simultaneously, disturbed youth are going into schools and public venues murdering fellow students, teachers, and innocent bystanders. Who has the solution? The #MeToo and #TimesUp movements are a wonderful start, but it's little more than a knee-jerk reaction to a situation that has been ongoing for centuries. What is the solution? Who will help the fallen men and women who have been committing these acts of violence and abuse, and the children, adolescents, and adults who were victimized?

Together, we will! And I will show you how. I am a former sex abuse survivor, a guy who once lived a homosexual life and is now married (believe it or not, my wife and I were married along with 2,100 couples in Madison Square Garden—yes, I was one of those so-called Moonies; we left them in 1995), and for a brief time while attending university in the 70s, I was a prostitute. I wanted to understand what people were looking for. What I found was quite simple—Time, Touch & Talk. Not really sex, but to be held, to be heard, and to be loved. I am not only an out-of-the-box person, I think, "What box?"

All these life experiences, combined with being a successful psychotherapist for over 30 years, allows me to understand the dark side of human nature, and the way to freedom and true intimacy. I will show you the path to fulfill your deepest desires in a most loving and beautiful way. Come with me on this journey, and I promise you will experience the beauty, love, and joy that exist deep within the depths of your heart and soul.

• •

> "Recent research in neuroscience has shown that loving touch is not an optional aspect of childrearing; it is essential for child development, and a lack of touch damages not only individuals, but our whole society. Loving touch releases the hormones oxytocin and dopamine, while infants who have not been touched have an increase in their levels of the stress hormone cortisol" (Braun, Ellen C. *Touch Hunger,* May 15, 2007. Retrieved from: http://raisingsmallsouls.com/touch-hunger/#respond).

• •

It is easy to unite people around a common enemy, for example, during wars, terrorist attacks or sex-abuse scandals. It is quite difficult to unite people for a positive cause. *We either change through crisis or conscious choice.* The latter is the most difficult and a road less traveled.

When was the last time someone touched you in a non-sexual way, looked into your eyes, saw you for who you genuinely are, and held you in their arms? When? We all crave intimacy. We are born with skin hunger, and most of us are hungry as hell for love.

Oftentimes, people have sex just to experience a morsel of touch and intimacy. And we enjoy a moment of touch when we go to the barber, hairdresser, chiropractor, doctor, nurse, massage therapist, and others.

Some go online to view Internet porn and masturbate, while others use apps to hook-up for sex, Tinder and Grindr to name just a few. Over the past few years, in preparation for writing this book, I did research by investigating an underground world. I found a subculture of men and women—many of whom are married—who hook up for a moment of pleasure, just to be held, or in most cases with men, just to get off, get out, and never to return because of guilt.

We need to introduce a radical paradigm shift in our culture and world—HEALTHY TOUCH HEALS. Say it over and over and over again: HEALTHY TOUCH HEALS. As the song says, "Reach out and touch somebody's hand, make this world a better place, if you can" (Nickolas Ashford and Valerie Simpson).

We can and must reverse this crisis by changing the equation. Solutions never come from within the system. Albert Einstein said, "No problem can be solved from the same level of consciousness that created it." In his book entitled *First Break All the Rules*, author Marcus Buckingham states, "Great leaders do not hesitate to break virtually every rule held sacred by conventional wisdom." We are at our best during a crisis—coming to the aid of our fellow men and women in need. And yet, we seem to be at our worst during normal times. Now is the occasion for a radical paradigm shift. It is time for TTT: to be held, to be heard, and to be loved.

There are hundreds of books on parenting and healing, and painfully few contain words about healthy touch. And yet the topic of touch is so, well, touchy, even when it relates to us with our own children. That's why some of us are raising detached children who may masturbate more, become violent, addicted to sex and/

or substances, and go through life empty and not know why. Basic unmet love needs for bonding in the early stages of child development will create a lifetime of deprivation unless someone steps in to help them, offering the gift of healthy touch. And don't be concerned if your children are older. I will provide many exercises for family healing and the use of healthy touch.

I have not mentioned the book's other two important themes, Time and Talk. In the section on Time, you will learn life-changing skills to become more powerful and peaceful in your personal and professional lives. The mastery of these skills will have a remarkable impact on your sense of wellbeing and success in all relationships. I am including the pearls, diamonds, and precious gems of therapeutic skills that I have acquired over the past thirty years. They will help save you time on your healing journey.

In the section on Talk, you will learn how to effectively share and listen, while learning to express yourself in more powerful ways in all relationships, both within and outside of your family. Additionally, you will come to understand how different personality styles impact our intimate relationships. With this important knowledge, you will gain a greater sense of understanding and respect for the different personalities of those you live and work with on a daily basis. What were once sources of contention will now become a sense of wonder and appreciation. "Aha! So that's how she perceives life!"

For these reasons, the book is divided into three sections: Time, Touch & Talk (TTT). Each section is divided into three sub-categories: Self-Healing, Family Healing, and Community Healing. After having written four books, I want to make this one succinct, full of practical tools for healing, amazing stories of transformation, and drawings, charts, and photos to simplify basic life-changing skills for yourself, your family, and community.

Be forewarned, I will repeat key concepts many times throughout the book. The more you read them, the greater the likelihood that these key concepts will enter your psyche.

Also, this is a workbook consisting of many exercises. To get the maximum benefit I suggest doing as many of these exercises as possible. Whether or not you are dealing with any particular problem or unresolved issue, the exercises will help bring resolution and greater peace in every aspect of your life—emotional, mental, physical, and spiritual.

Change occurs not through reading alone, but through *practicing* skills repeatedly. Finally, when you have finished reading the book, I hope you will start from the beginning once again. I promise that upon each reading you will learn even more new lessons of love that will last a lifetime. And if you are in a relationship, why not do the exercises together? It will foster greater understanding, love, and intimacy.

So to sum up, this book is Phase One to promote an understanding of our undeniable need for healthy Time, Touch & Talk on a regular basis. In the conclusion, I will share an exciting vision about Phase Two: TTT centers throughout the world.

---

*There are many psychological concepts and exercises introduced throughout the book. For a greater understanding of these principles of healing, please see the list of references at the back of the book for further study.

Prologue

Once upon a time, oh yes, the world was beautiful … you would have loved it. The trees were bursting with fresh, ripe fruit. The smell of wild flowers filled the air. Two magnificent looking people—a handsome man and a beautiful woman—walked upon the face of the earth. They merrily ate and drank. Day after day, they enjoyed exploring their world together. Oh, and did I forget to mention? They were both naked and unashamed.

Their fun-filled lives consisted of strolling, running, and exploring the wild. Every day was a feast of the senses. They worked without stress while interacting with nature. They were alive! They were free! They simply enjoyed the many pleasures that God had created just for them.

And they were whole. They were in touch with themselves, each other, and the earth. They communed with nature, and shared their garden with countless beautiful animals. They felt what God felt. They freely shared with Him and each other. There were no walls around their hearts. No barriers around their minds. Race, religion, politics, industry, entertainment, education were of no concern to them—in fact they didn't exist. The lovely couple breathed fresh, clean, pure air as they wandered, unclothed and uninhibited, throughout paradise.

And then boom! The reverie ended. It stopped. Next thing you know, they were covering up their private parts! Concealing their genitals. Why? What went wrong? Why were they hiding in the bushes? Who were they hiding from? What had they done that was so bad they had to cover themselves up and hide?

We have been paying for that event ever since—whether an actual event or a metaphor—which is spoken about in the book of Genesis. Most cultures, faiths, and civilizations have similar stories of a *fall from grace* which led to guilt, shame, fear, blame, anger, murder, abuse, violence, and death. These are the bitter fruits which we've inherited from our first family!

Once upon a time there was Paradise. Then Paradise was lost. Since then, we have been passionately pursuing Paradise—through personal achievements, sensual gratification, and often times failed relationships. Since that fall from grace, the greatest and most precious things were confounded: sex, love, and intimacy. These three became separated and all *meshed up.** History has recorded men's desperate attempts to undo this mesh. God, making numerous pleas throughout His-story, has worked tirelessly to awaken our hearts and minds to live in truth with love.

I am a simple man from a meshed up past who has learned many lessons through countless mistakes and victories. My passion is to see the world healed through healthy Time, Touch & Talk (TTT). I know that it is possible. If a broken soul such as I can be restored, then I know for certain that anyone is capable of living a life of real love.

Like a different kind of Happy Hour (a period when discount drinks are available in bars), we will create a safe place for healthy Time, Touch & Talk—to be held, to be heard, and to be loved (more about this in the conclusion of the book). TTT is a revolution of real love whose time has come. It has been said that the pen is mightier than the sword. So I pray this book ignites a revolution of TTT real love throughout the world. [T³ = two people sharing TTT, creating a synergistic effect!]

TTT is a simple yet profound blueprint to recreate a new paradise on earth, or at least it's a start. Please join with me in practicing the simple skills I will describe in the pages that follow in order to achieve your hearts' desire. I am looking forward to traveling together alongside you!

*I am taking the concept of enmeshment (inappropriate boundaries in relationships, or entanglement) and being messed up, and created the new word "mesh" or "meshed up!"

TIME, TOUCH & TALK

By Richard Cohen, M.A. © 2019

TIME	TOUCH	TALK
Time = Love Sunlight Affirmation Competency	Healthy touch = Love Water Affection Belonging	Listening & sharing = Love Air Acceptance Value
Time with God, self, others, and nature. Time is an investment of love. Activities: play, games, fun, sports, arts, walks, camping, fishing, exploring. Fun times together: create memories. Inner Child come out and play! Skills to resolve negative thoughts: Affirmations. Healing Wounds and fulfilling unmet love needs in healthy, non-sexual relationships.	Bonding rituals: cuddling, hugging, kissing, smiling, eye contact. Secure attachment in primary family relationships creates a sense of self-worth and success in personal and professional life. Touch ≠ Sex Affairs (hetero/homo) outside of marriage, porn, compulsive masturbation—are all false attempts to heal wounds and fulful unmet love needs. We recreate our past in present relationships in order to bring resolution and reconciliation. We want to be loved for who we *are*, not what we *do*. Healthy hugs; holding, embracing and other therapeutic exercises. Children, adolescents, adults need healthy touch on a daily basis to survive and thrive. 6 D's: Divorce, Daycare, Digital Technology, Decline of values, Dysfunction, and Detached children looking for love in wrong ways and in wrong places.	Communication skills—effective listening and sharing; variety of skills for intimacy. KYMS: Keep Your Mouth Shut; just listen; join the other; learn to express your feelings, thought, and needs. You won't get it, if you don't ask for it. Expectations Kill! Different personality types: Myers-Briggs, Enneagram, Four temperaments, Love Languages, Birth order. Take ownership of your thoughts, feelings, and needs. The only true response to another is love. Everything else is fear, or lack of love. Moving from disgust to compassion; embracing differences.

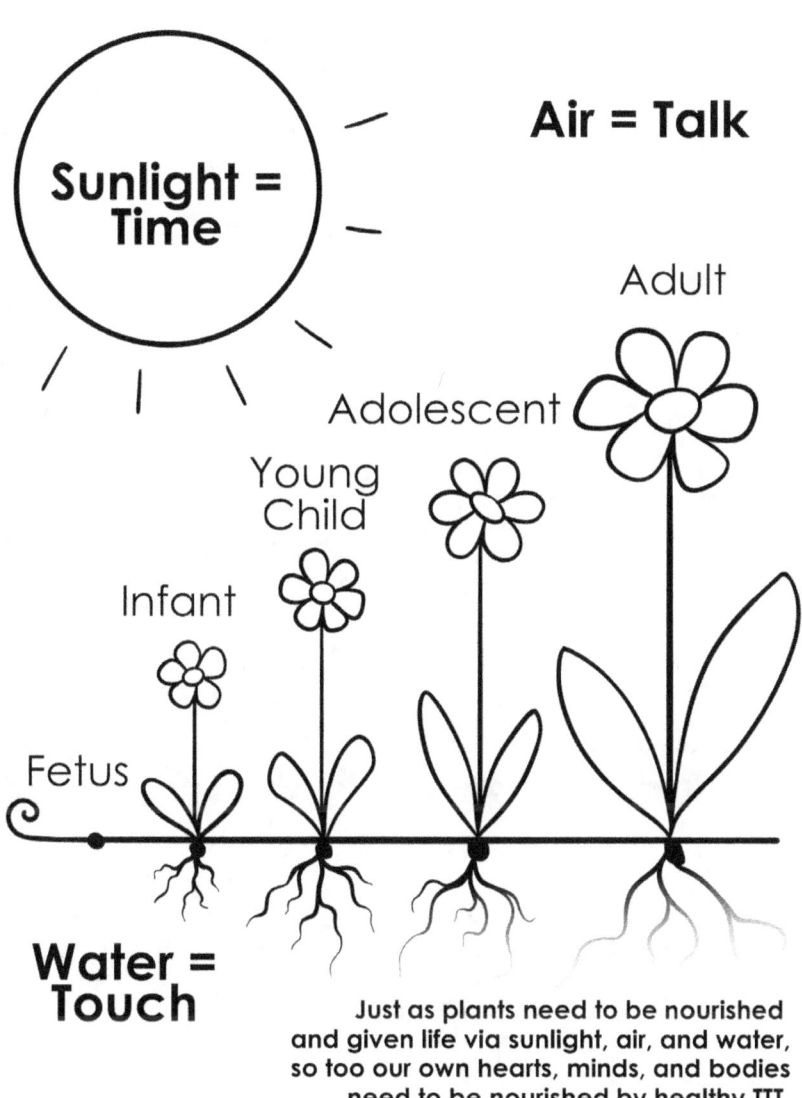

Section One—Time

TIME represents sunlight. The sun provides light energy, a process called photosynthesis, for plants to grow. And now it is Time to get in touch with your soul, to heal your wounds, and to fulfill your unmet love needs. No one will love and respect you if you don't love and respect yourself.[1] World peace begins one person at a time, with each of us. Self-hatred works its way outward, affecting all of our personal and professional relationships. Hurting people hurt people. Self-love also extends outward.

---

1 There are many ways to view people who appear weak or wounded. Here are a few approaches:

1) Dr. Greg Bear, in his book *Real Love*, states that if someone is behaving poorly or defensively, s/he is employing getting and protecting behaviors—attempting to mask emptiness and/or fear which comes from their deep-seated insecurities and unmet love needs. Realize that they are in pain and show them greater love as you are able.

2) Johann Wolfgang von Goethe's approach is to look at another person who doesn't love himself or herself and envision greatness for him or her. Goethe, a poet, novelist, playwright, and statesman said, "If you treat an individual as he is, he will remain as he is. But if you treat him as if he were what he ought to be and could be, he will become what he ought to be and could be." Therefore see the hurting person in your mind's eye, through the lens of your heart, and speak life into his or her life either silently to yourself or in spoken words. "I see you as an amazing woman. I understand that you are not feeling well or are in pain. I see beyond this experience and witness your infinite beauty and brilliance."

3) Toby Mac, Christian Hip-Hop musician, sings in his song "Speak Life" the following sentiment: "Look into the eyes of the broken hearted, watch them come alive as soon as you speak hope, you speak love, you speak life." These suggestions may or may not work, depending on the openness or woundedness of the other person.

HEALING HUMANITY: TIME, TOUCH & TALK

Love is Spelled Time, a song by Brent Henderson

"I used to have a best friend, when I was growing up,
I remember when he showed, his brand new baseball glove.
I thought he was so lucky, until I heard him say:
I wish my Dad would take the time, and teach me how to play.

"Love is spelled time, Love is spelled time.
It's something you spend, not something you buy.
Before it's too late, I hope you will find.
In the eyes of child, love is spelled time."

Let me share with you some wonderful exercises for self-healing, family healing, and community healing.

• •

The best gift you can give your partner and children is to heal yourself. Otherwise you pass on to the next generation all the unresolved issues of your past. Leave a legacy of real love for your children and grandchildren by healing yourself.

• •

TIME

Self-Healing

- Feelings Wheel
- Potential Causes of Wounding
- Layers of Our Personality
- Support Network
- Cognitive Changes
- Affirmations
- Inner Child Healing

Family Healing

- New Map for Your Family: 13 Rs
- Twelve people in One Marriage!
- Family Fun Exercises

Community Healing

- Spend Time with Friends
- Time for Your Passions
- Volunteer in Your Community

Self-Healing

Do you remember those famous words from the movie Jerry McGuire, "You complete me?" That very idea is absolute nonsense and a formula for failure in all relationships! Such a concept leads to codependency and ultimately a miserable life and potential divorce. If he completes her, she is ready to be rejected at any moment, and he holds the power for her happiness and misery in his hands. In that simple statement, "You complete me," someone seizes authority over another's wellbeing while the other person is giving their power away. Don't become a victim, vulnerable and easily hurt. Do not give your power away to anyone! If you try to create intimacy with another person before you complete the process of becoming your best self, all relationships become an attempt to fill your void. No one can complete you. They may, however, **complement** you!

You can complete yourself through personal healing activities and exercises. I will suggest many practical tools throughout the book. You are magnificent and destined for greatness. I know this because you are created as a unique manifestation of God's love and truth. But first things first: heal yourself. Then you may *complement* your partner. If you are already in a relationship, get started now. It's never too late. "Life can only be understood backwards; but it must be lived forwards," stated Danish philosopher and theologian Soren Kierkegaard. Perhaps you don't yet have all the answers or solutions, but just keep going and growing, and keep trying until you get there. Mistakes are how we learn.

We don't know what we don't know. We fear that which we don't understand, and we unconsciously resurrect our past wounds and unmet love needs in present day personal and professional relationships. Two pillars—unhealed wounds and unmet love needs from the past—drive our unwanted behaviors, i.e., compulsive masturbation, affairs, addictions. TTT is the solution. There are very meaningful and specific purposes for TTT: to help us heal our hearts, and to fulfill basic love needs in healthy, non-sexual relationships. Healthy touch is the missing link in all facets of our lives: family, friends, work, faith, and community.

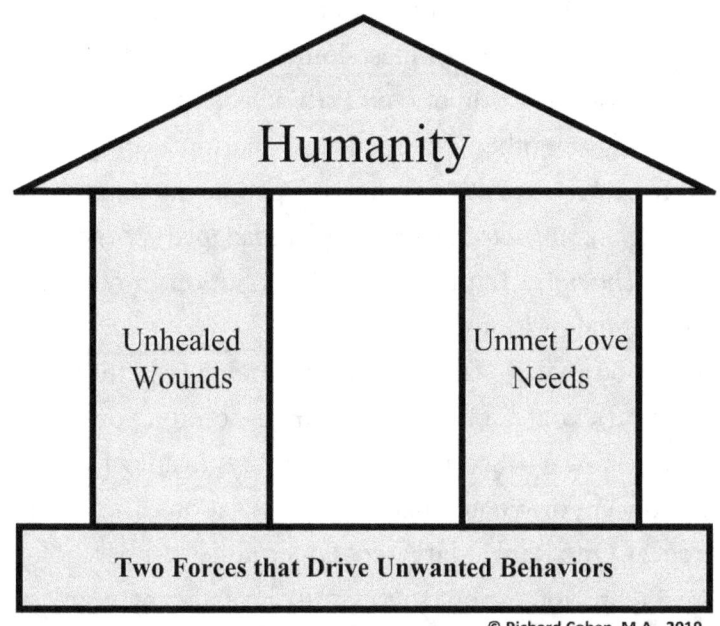

© Richard Cohen, M.A., 2019

• •

You are not responsible *for* someone, you are responsible *to* them—to be honest, loving, and genuine. If you believe that you are responsible *for* someone's feelings, you will shrink from being yourself in life.

• •

Most movies seem to show us that violence wins wars. Yet history teaches us that wars won through violence are temporary; the results *never* last. We must embrace our anger, our inner bastard or our inner bitch. We must understand our wounded hearts. The real battlefield today is within each one of us.

I call the pattern of unnecessary violence and loss *The Romeo & Juliet Principle*. Remember William Shakespeare's play *Romeo & Juliet*? Through the death of their children, the Capulets and Montagues finally united. It took bloodshed to create breakthrough. However, this is unnecessary if we begin a Time, Touch & Talk program in our families, communities, and culture. We may actually rid the world of *Pain Pollution* by spending time with ourselves and each other. I define Pain Pollution as projecting our unresolved issues onto others—hurting people hurting other people. Once again, *unhealed wounds and unmet love needs drive most unwanted behaviors*. The result is Pain Pollution in our personal and professional relationships.

Unless you make peace with your parents (whether they are living or dead), you can never leave home—even if you live thousands of miles away—because they are always inside of you.

This concept originated from Object Relations Theory of Sandor Ferenczi, Otto Rank, Margaret Mahler, and other psychologists. If you're a man, you cannot successfully love a woman unless you love your mother (or resolve your issues with her and experience healthy feminine love from others). If you're a woman, you cannot successfully love a man unless you love your father (or resolve your issues with him and experience healthy love from other men).

Negative bonding patterns from your past are forever projected onto present relationships unless resolved. We relate to those of the opposite sex as we did with our (either loved or abhorred) parents. Hatred and hurt works its way outward. *We must feel and be real in order to heal.* Grieve the losses of your past so that you may be healthy in present day relationships. If you ignore this process, and continue projecting your wounds onto those around you, you are increasing PAIN POLLUTION throughout the world. Worse than environmental pollution, is Pain Pollution. TTT will begin a revolution to resolve Pain Pollution around the globe.

Feelings Wheel*

It is very important that we learn to identify what we are *thinking*, what we are *feeling*, and what we *need*. Otherwise, we remain at the mercy of others to create our sense of wellbeing. There are many versions of the Feeling Wheel available on the Internet. I like the version that I've reproduced below because it clearly differentiates between our core emotions (experienced in the amygdala and limbic system) and our feeling responses (experienced in the neocortex). Emotions are coded in our genes and were created to reward (pleasure responses) or to protect (fight, flight, or freeze). Feelings are a combination of our experiences, thoughts, judgments, and opinions. Core emotions are love, anger, and fear. All other responses are feelings, which depend upon our love needs being met or unmet.

Bret Stein, creator of the Feelings Wheel, explains, "There are many researchers who study human emotions, and they are not all in agreement with what constitutes an emotion, as well as how many different emotions exist. The Feelings Wheel is organized based on Paul Ekman's research into the six emotions that he has demonstrated to be universally recognizable by most people across all cultures, largely due to the uniformity of facial muscles that contract when these emotions are experienced. The six emotions are anger, disgust, fear, happiness, sadness, and surprise. I chose to use these six feelings and their opposites to construct the Feelings Wheel."

Stein continues, "Not all emotions elicit an observable facial expression, and Ekman believes there are probably 15 to 20 'basic' emotions in all. Each emotion does elicit a varied physiological response, and is believed to activate a separate and distinct area of the brain. Brain imaging techniques such as functional MRI are now being used to research these emotions. Ekman's work is quite fascinating, and he produces material and resources on how to identify and recognize different human emotions, which he uses to train counselors, teachers, parents, policemen, and secret service agents. (www.paulekman.com). John Cleese (of Monty Python fame) stars in a funny BBC educational video called *The Human Face* which describes some of Ekman's work.

"Other authors who have worked with Ekman and refer to his work are Malcolm Gladwell in the book *Blink*; Daniel Goleman in *Emotional Intelligence, Social Intelligence and Destructive Emotions*; the Dalai Lama in *Emotional Awareness*; and John Gottman in *Raising Emotionally Intelligent Children*, and the *10 Emotions Feeling Identification Postcards* (www.talaris.org or www.gottman.com). I mention these authors as I suspect anyone interested in learning and using NVC (Nonviolent Communication) may also be interested in the resources these authors have made available."

Learn to use this Feelings Wheel daily to help you identify your experiences at any given moment. Become the master of your own ship by taking responsibility for your feeling responses in each of your personal and professional relationships. If you are married, practice this with your partner and children. It may be a fun activity for all your family to learn together. A simple exercise to use regularly with your partner and/or family is this:

1) Name two feeling words that best represent how you are in the moment
2) Share what is behind your two feeling words
3) Express a need that you may have, either from your partner and/or children

SECTION ONE—TIME

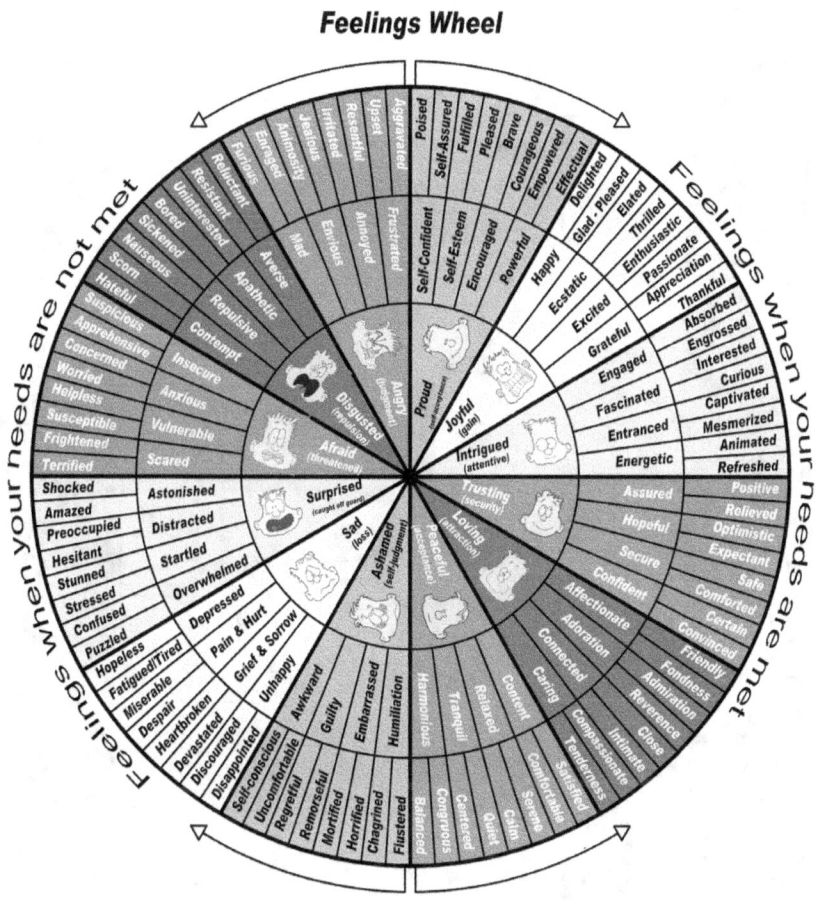

Feelings are *internal* emotions. Words mistaken for emotions, but that are actually thoughts in the form of evaluations and judgments of others, are any words that follow "I feel like ... " or "I feel that ..." or "I feel as if ... " or "I feel you ...", such as:

Abandoned	Attacked	Abused	Betrayed	Blamed	Bullied	Cheated
Coerced	Criticized	Dismissed	Disrespected	Excluded	Ignored	Intimidated
Insulted	Let Down	Manipulated	Misunderstood	Neglected	Put down	Rejected
Unappreciated	Unloved	Unheard	Unwanted	Used	Violated	Wronged

*Feelings Wheel used by permission from Bret Stein based on Nonviolent Communication (NVC).

Potential Causes of Wounding in Men & Women

Potential Causes of Wounding in Men & Women

Heredity	Temperament	Hetero-Emotional Wounds	Homo-Emotional Wounds	Sibling Wounds/ Family Dynamics	Body Image Wounds	Sexual Abuse	Social or Peer Wounds	Cultural Influences	Others Factors
Generational blessings and curses	Hypersensitive	Over-attachment to opposite-sex parent	Over-attachment to same-sex parent	Abuse: mental, emotional, physical, and/or sexual	Late bloomer	Premature sexualization	Name-calling	Internet porn	Divorce
Unresolved family issues	Artistic	Lack of attachment to opposite-sex parent	Lack of attachment to same-sex parent	Don't fit in	Physical disabilities	Heterosexual or homosexual imprinting	Put-downs	Media/ Entertainment Industry promoting sex	Death
Men resenting women, women resenting men	Four temperaments: Sanguine Choleric Melancholic Phlegmatic	Abuse: mental, emotional, physical, and/or sexual	Abuse: mental, emotional, physical, and/or sexual	Don't belong	Shorter / Taller	Learned/ reinforced behavior	Teacher's pet	Sexualizing legitimate needs for love	Suicide
Addictions: substances, sex, gambling	Enneagram	Parentified child: role reversal between parent and child	Parentified child: role reversal between parent and child	Different from others	Heavier / Thinner	Sex used as a substitute for love	Goody-goody		Addictions: alcohol, drugs, sex, gambling, etc.
Medical/Mental health issues	Extrovert / Introvert			Bullying / verbal abuse	Skin color issues		Nerd		Intra-uterine experience: insecure attachment
Financial problems							Non-athletic		Adoption
Predilection for rejection							Lack of gender identification and/or gender non-conforming behaviors		War/genocide
Racial, religious, ethnic prejudice									Religion: toxic beliefs

The severity of wounding in each category will have a direct impact on the amount of time and effort it will take to heal.

© Richard Cohen, M.A., 2019

Here is a list, not at all exhaustive, composed of many common issues that you may have experienced while growing up. Each potential cause may become a wound if you lived in an environment where such issues were not addressed and/or your gifts were not appreciated or accepted:

1. Heredity

- Generational blessings and curses
- Unresolved family issues
- Men resenting women, women resenting men
- Addictions: substances, sex, gambling
- Medical/Mental Health issues
- Financial problems
- Predilection for rejection
- Racial, religious, ethnic prejudice

Our parents' and grandparents' unresolved issues do not disappear. They are passed down from generation to generation until someone takes personal responsibility. The science of Epigenetics supports how our behavior and lifestyle affect how our genes express themselves (90% of genes turn on and off according to our behavior, environment, thinking, etc.). That's how predispositions toward things like alcoholism, are passed on.

Many of us have recognized how we repeat the emotional patterns we learned at home. We declare, "I will never act like my father or mother. I will never treat my spouse or children like they did." But then we find ourselves behaving in the same manner. Darn! Sexual abuse, resentment towards others, misuse of money are just a few issues that are passed on for generations. Hurts and hatred of our predecessors do not vanish, even if we say we love God. Salvation (God's gift to us) and sanctification (our lifelong healing process) are two very different issues.

My father and his sister fought with each other about money their entire lives. My aunt was fun and fantastic. Yet we were prohibited from seeing or speaking to her as she fell in and out of grace with my dad. My brother inherited many of these issues. He cut himself off from my sister and myself years ago.

Curses and blessings are real. The sins of our fathers and mothers, and past generations, need to be dealt with in order for our children to experience more freedom. For this reason, I decided to resolve the wounds of my past, so that my children would have a leg up on their journey in life. I did not want to pass on to them as much pain as I had experienced while growing up. I am sure my father and mother thought the same. As my brother-in-law once said, "We each try to make it a little easier for our children." The exercises that follow will allow you to break family curses and create new and loving patterns for the coming generations.

2. Temperament

- Hypersensitive
- Artistic
- Four temperaments: Sanguine (social, active) / Choleric (independent, decisive) / Melancholic (feeler, deep thinker) / Phlegmatic (peaceful, quiet)
- Enneagram (Reformer, Helper, Achiever, Individualist, Investigator, Loyalist, Enthusiast, Challenger, Peacemaker)
- Extrovert / Introvert

Each of us is endowed by our Creator with certain gifts and talents. If we live in a supportive environment while growing up, those gifts are fostered, and we grow to become who we are meant to be. If we live in an environment of criticism and judgment, then our gifts go underground, and we learn to simply survive the intolerable.

In our efforts toward healing, our talents and innate temperament will need to be unearthed, recovered, and restored. There are a variety of paradigms when it comes to diverse temperaments; some are mentioned above, and more will be defined in the Talk section. The main point is to identify your temperament and foster those gifts as you grow to be the best version of yourself.

3. Hetero-Emotional Wounds

- Over-attachment to opposite-sex parent
- Lack of attachment to opposite-sex parent
- Abuse: mental, emotional, physical, and/or sexual
- Parentified child: role reversal between parent and child

Father-daughter and mother-son relationships are essential for healthy growth into womanhood or manhood. As a woman, if your father was unavailable, abusive, or insulting to your mother, this may have led to the wounding of your own femininity and the feeling of safety with men. As a man, if your mother leaned on you, was unavailable as the primary source of feminine love, and/or was critical and judgmental, then your heart will need to recover from those wounds. Ultimately, you need to forgive her and experience beautiful feminine love, from her or healthy women. A single parent must play the role of both father and mother, which may negatively impact the child. Unresolved wounds become our unconscious agenda for all personal and professional relationships. We will treat others as we were treated unless we work it out. We may seek love and approval from others of the opposite sex in an oftentimes unconscious attempt to win our father's or mother's love.

4. Homo-Emotional Wounds

- Over-attachment to same-sex parent
- Lack of attachment to same-sex parent
- Abuse: mental, emotional, physical, and/or sexual
- Parentified child: role reversal between parent and child

A boy gains his sense of masculinity from his father during the first years of his life. In preadolescence, he experiences a sense of gender identity by playing with male relatives and peers. Then he belongs to the tribe of men. A girl inherits her sense of femininity first from her mother, and then from other girls (female relatives and friends in preadolescence).

If the father and son had different temperaments, and the dad was critical and rejecting of his son, this may damage the boy's sense of masculinity, and/or he may develop a layer of toughness so that no one may get close to him. If the mother and her daughter were extremely different in temperaments, if the mother rejected or criticized her daughter, if the mother was aloof and detached, any of these and more circumstances will create a vacuum in the daughter's soul, leaving a void to be filled. These and other wounds must be addressed, or they may have life-damaging consequences.

My Little Golden Book About GOD offers a lovely portrait: "God is the love of our mother's kiss, and the warm, strong hug of our daddy's arms." Pictured are both Father and Mother holding their children. Parents are God's representatives to their children. When children detach from either Mr. or Mrs. God, they are distancing themselves from their role models of gender identification. Therefore, a defensive detachment—erecting walls around one's heart—from father and/or mother may lead to a defensive detachment toward God.

5. Sibling Wounds / Family Dynamics

- Abuse: mental, emotional, physical, and/or sexual
- Don't fit in
- Don't belong
- Different from others
- Bullying / verbal abuse

If your brother mocked you, if your sister picked on you, if your cousins criticized you, if you were always the odd one out, these and other experiences within the family system create deep wounds in your soul. These issues do not disappear until they are extracted and replaced with positive affirmations and healthy relationships.

6. Body Image Wounds

- Late bloomer
- Physical disabilities
- Shorter / Taller
- Heavier / Thinner
- Skin color issues

Being a "late bloomer," experiencing early maturation or a physical disability, being shorter, taller, thinner, or larger—these are some characteristics that may result in body image wounds. Bodily attributes may cause pain because of peer or parental reactions. Many, if not all, of those I've counseled have felt a lower sense of self-worth due to feelings of inadequacy about his or her physical appearance.

In adolescence, some didn't develop as quickly as others and therefore felt inferior to their peers. Others were either overweight or extremely thin, which contributed to a sense of low self-worth.

Others were shorter, never grew as tall as their peers, and were left feeling inadequate and insecure, while others were much taller than their peers and were mocked for this. Others may have had some kind of physical disability and received or perceived social criticism and rejection. Still others may have been told or perceived they were not as attractive as their siblings or peers. With social media and advertisements promoting photos of air-brushed models and movie stars, we all fall short of unobtainable images, and that can leave us feeling insecure and "less than" others.

Skin color is a deep source of wounding for many throughout the world. Having different pigmentation from the majority of the population may create feelings of inferiority or the experience of prejudice, or internalized guilt and shame (which is more insidious). Even within one's race, having a lighter or darker skin tone creates barriers and often grounds for superiority or inferiority. This sense of being different needs to be resolved, otherwise it lays the groundwork for continued hurt and pain.

7. Sexual Abuse

- Premature sexualization
- Heterosexual or homosexual imprinting
- Learned/reinforced behavior
- Sex used as a substitute for love

In the U.S.A., research shows that approximately one in every three to four girls and one in every five to six boys experienced childhood sexual abuse. The statistics and definitions of sexual abuse varies from state to state, and country to country. However, the implication is that an older person takes advantage of the trust and vulnerability of a younger person. Those who did not securely attach and connect with their parent(s) are much more vulnerable to the influence of a perpetrator. Research indicates that every perpetrator was once a victim of childhood abuse. Sexual abuse is not really about sex, but power. The perpetrator is re-enacting what she or he experienced. This generational travesty does not disappear with faith, fame, or fortune. Only by addressing the issue directly, and by healing the deep wounds and scars are we able to become free, and help end this pattern of violation.

Sexual predators can easily perceive unmet emotional needs in a child or adolescent. Most often, the perpetrators of sexual abuse are family members or close friends of the family. The insidious nature of abuse is that it often begins as emotional intimacy and later becomes sexual. The perpetrator gains the trust of the child, fulfilling basic love needs for acceptance. Then he alters the relationship to include sex. This is a very confusing message to a needy and impressionable child. Here, the psychic wiring and physiology of the child become confused and meshed up because the messages of love, sex, and intimacy become intertwined.

8. Social or Peer Wounds

- Name-calling
- Put-downs
- Teacher's pet
- Goody-goody
- Nerd
- Non-athletic
- Lack of gender identification and/or gender non-conforming behaviors

"Sticks and stones may break my bones, but names will never hurt me" is a big lie. Bones and skin heal rather quickly, but the psychic wounds left by name calling last a lifetime unless extracted from our souls. Additionally, if we did not conform to gender norms—such as the more sensitive boy and the more athletic girl—then we may also have been teased and mocked. We must reclaim our power and bathe in the joy of being who we were meant to be.

According to the Pew Research Center, almost 60% of teens have experienced cyberbullying, with name-calling and rumor-spreading being the most common forms of harassment ("A Majority of Teens Have Experienced Some Form of Cyberbullying" survey March 7-April 10, 2018). Tweens (middle-school children) are often the victims of bullying at school or through social media. These experiences lead to depression, low self-worth, and in some cases suicidal ideation. Whether in current times or in days past, many of us have experienced some form of bullying and being different from the pack.

"Fathers may influence children in ways that mothers don't, particularly in areas such as the child's peer relationships and achievement at school. Research indicates, for example, that boys with absent fathers have a harder time finding a balance between masculine assertiveness and self-restraint. Consequently, it's tougher for them to learn self-control and to delay gratification—skills that become increasingly important as boys grow and reach out for friendship, academic success, and career goals. A father's positive presence can be a significant factor in a girl's academic and career achievement as well, although the evidence here is more ambiguous. It's clear, however, that girls whose fathers are present and involved in their lives are less likely to become sexually promiscuous at a young age, and more likely to forge healthy relationships with men when they become adults" (Gottman, John, *The Heart of Parenting*, New York: Simon and Schuster, 1977, page 166).

9. Cultural influences

- Internet porn
- Media/Entertainment Industry promoting sex
- Sexualizing legitimate needs for love

Today we are inundated with sexual images that may influence us to do that which we do not want to do. If these sexual images continue to overwhelm our culture/society, eventually they become the norm, and our brain circuitry is rewired. By sexualizing another person, we block our deeper needs for real relationships and true intimacy. On the Internet, a young child may view pornography, seeing every imaginable and unimaginable sexual act between two adults, male or female or a variation of genders. This is abuse of our children's minds.

10. Other Factors

- Divorce
- Death
- Suicide
- Addictions: alcohol, drugs, sex, gambling, etc.
- Intra-uterine experience: insecure attachment
- Adoption
- War/genocide
- Religion: toxic beliefs

If his parents divorced, a son may blame himself. "If only I had been a better child they would have stayed together." If a parent dies, a daughter may blame herself. "It's all my fault." This of course is an unconscious message buried deep in her psyche. If a parent or close relative commits suicide, once again, self-blame may result. If a parent is addicted to a substance or behavior, children are led to believe that their feelings, thoughts, and needs are unimportant, as the family system revolves around the addict and enabler.

Pre-natal psychology has conducted research detailing the mother's, and secondarily the father's, thoughts and feelings influence upon the unborn child. Please read Dr. Thomas Verny's insightful book for more details: *The Secret Life of the Unborn Child*.

Adopted children may unconsciously reject their new parents believing, "I am unwanted by my biological parents and therefore I don't believe anyone will ever love me." The experience of being raised in wartime greatly impacts parents and children, "Life is not safe."

If someone grows up with a judgmental, toxic spiritual belief system, i.e. "You are bad and sinful for…," or "You are being disobedient to God's word," a danger may arise: "God rejects me for who I am." Those kinds of theo-pathological beliefs have consequences that may last a lifetime. "I'm no good." "Who can accept me for who I am?" "I'm unforgiveable."

These ten influences—*heredity, temperament, hetero-emotional wounds, homo-emotional wounds, sibling wounds/family dynamics, body-image wounds, sexual abuse, social or peer wounds, cultural wounds,* and *other factors: divorce/death/intrauterine experiences/adoption/religion*—represent major factors of wounding in men and women.

Exercise

Using these ten potential causes of wounding, and any other hurtful experiences not mentioned, make a list of issues that you experienced while growing up: issues that you have resolved, and others yet to be solved. This will become your agenda for personal healing.

By addressing each one of these issues, by uncovering their meaning and impact, you may heal and achieve your full potential. *The severity of wounding in each category will have a direct impact on the amount of time and effort it will take to heal.*

• •

> "Each of us enters adulthood harboring unresolved childhood issues with our parents, whether or not we know it or will admit it. Those needs have to be met, because their satisfaction is equated, in our unconscious minds, with survival. Therefore, their satisfaction becomes the agenda in adult love relationships" (Hendrix, Harville, *Getting the Love You Want: A Couples' Study Guide*, New York: Harper Perennial, 1988, page 26).

• •

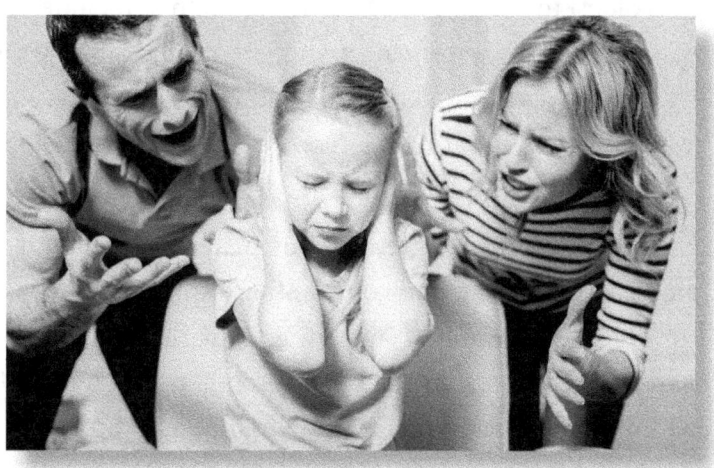

Exercise

After completing your list of potential wounds, draw a *genogram* of three generations (see the example below). A genogram is another name for a family tree or a map of three generations. This is a very important exercise to help you identify patterns in relationships that have been passed down from one generation to the next. This will help you further identify the secret ties that bind (positive and negative generational bonding patterns), begin to heal your wounds, and make constructive changes in your life.

When speaking with your family members, do so in a very compassionate and curious manner. Your parents or grandparents (if they are living) may become defensive if they think you are interrogating or judging them. Simply say that you are interested in the family history for your own personal growth and healing. Here is a suggested list of questions to help you construct your genogram or family tree:

Section One:

1. Name your father's parents (your paternal grandfather and grandmother) and name your father's siblings in birth order from oldest to youngest, including your father. Include the year that each person was born (grandparents and siblings). Identify who is/was married to whom, and who might have passed away. Also include if there were any miscarriages, stillbirths, abortions, or if a child died.

2. Name your mother's parents (your maternal grandfather and grandmother) and name your mother's siblings in birth order from oldest to youngest, including your mother. Include the year that each person was born (grandparents and siblings). Identify who is/was married to whom, and who might have

SECTION ONE—TIME

passed away. Also include if there were any miscarriages, stillbirths, abortions, or if a child died.

3. Names, birth years, and children that your parents had (your siblings and you). List if your siblings are married, and their spouses' name(s), and number of children. Include the age, name, and gender of each of your children. If there was a miscarriage, stillbirths, abortions, or child died, please include each of them as well. List their birth order, year they were born, or passed away.

Section Two:

1. Describe the relationship between your father and his father, your father and his mother, your father and his siblings (if he had any), and your father and any other significant people in his life while he was growing up. Include the names and birth order of all your father's siblings.
2. Describe the relationship between your father's parents—past to present.
3. Where did your father's family live? Where did he grow up?
4. What was their ethnic background? What was their religious background?
5. Describe the relationship between your mother and her father, your mother and her mother, your mother and her siblings, and any other significant people in her life growing up. Include the names and birth order of all your mother's siblings.
6. Describe the relationship between your mother's parents—past to present.
7. Where did your mother's family live? Where did she grow up?

8. What was their ethnic background? Religious background?
9. Be sure to describe any major issues or events on both the paternal and maternal sides of the family, such as war experiences, immigration, sexual abuse, physical abuse, emotional-mental abuse, drug/alcohol/sexual addictions, gambling addictions, eating disorders, sexual problems, major depressions, divorce, suicide, rape, murder, theft, abortions, homosexuality, adoption, moving, etc.

Section Three:

1. Describe your relationship with your father—past (from your earliest memories) to the present (current-day relationship).
2. Describe your father's personality—past to present.
3. Describe your father's education, employment history, and religious history.
4. Describe your relationship with your mother—past to present.
5. Describe your mother's personality—past to present.
6. Describe your mother's education, employment history, and religious history.
7. Describe the relationship between your father and mother—past to present.
8. Describe your relationship with your siblings (if you have any)—past to present.
9. Describe your siblings' personalities.
10. Describe your relationship with any other significant people in or out of your family system (e.g., grandmother, grandfather, uncle, cousin, neighbor, stepparent).

SECTION ONE—TIME

11. What was your role in the family system (e.g., hero, pleaser, clown, rebel, substitute spouse, golden child, caretaker, loner, scapegoat, peacemaker)?

12. Describe your school history—academically and socially, past to present.

13. Describe your new family:
    a. Personality of your spouse
    b. Name and personality of each of your children (year of birth)

14. Describe any other influential people in the lives of your children while they were growing up.

15. Describe any other important events in your life and the lives of your children while they were growing up.

16. Describe your religious history and that of your family.

17. Describe yourself—how you see yourself today.

18. List any other significant issues about your life or your family that were not covered in these questions, such as health issues, marriage issues, extramarital affairs, career issues, or money issues.

Exercise

Draw your genogram.

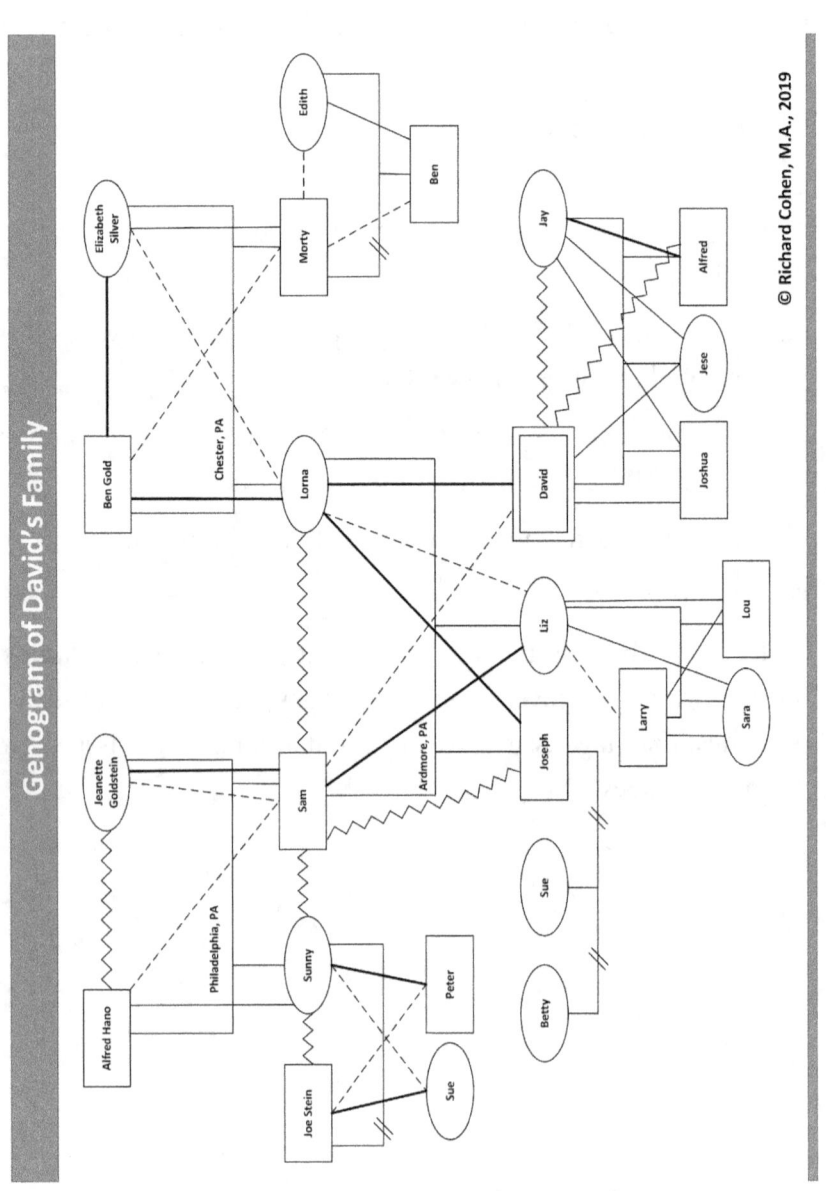

SECTION ONE—TIME

List of symbols:

- Circles represent women and squares represent men.
- An X through a person means they have passed away.
- A double diagonal line means this couple has separated or divorced. Place this symbol closer to the parent with whom the children are *not* living. For example, if the parents divorced, and the children live with their mother, then the double line is placed next to the father.
- If a father was close to his daughter, make the line connecting them very strong (thicker than a normal line).
- If a mother was distant or detached from her daughter, make it a dotted line, representing a lack of connection.
- If a parent was abusive to a child, make the line dotted and jagged, representing some form of abuse (physical, emotional, mental, and/or sexual)
- If the parents' relationship is close, make a thick line between them.
- If the parents' relationship was distant, make it a dotted line between them.
- If the parents' relationship was abusive, i.e. arguments, fights, and lack of intimacy, making it a jagged line, representing conflict.
- Oldest child is on the left, then the next oldest until the youngest is on the far right.
- You may use a diamond symbol to represent pets, if this animal was an important part of the family system.

Once again, the purpose of creating your genogram or family tree is to see the bigger picture, positive and negative generational bonding patterns. We may have experienced wounding from our parents, relatives, peers, and additionally inherited unresolved issues from previous generations. These issues do not disappear.

*Time alone does not heal anything,
it only buries the unresolved issues deeper!*

God has provided us with the natural process of healing. *It is called grieving.* When a child gets hurt (physically or emotionally), she or he cries. Children need to be comforted, held, and if there is a physical wound, tended to and mended. Then off they go with joy and gratitude. This is the natural process of healing. However, if we experienced emotional hurts in our hearts that were not heard and healed, we have learned to cope by developing layers of protection.

Layers of Our Personality

At the core of our being is our God-given self, full of love, understanding, and forgiveness. We also come into the world with an inherited self, a combination of our ancestors' victories and failures (Transgenerational Family Therapy and Epigenetics).

In the first years of life, if we experienced or perceived any kind of wounding—abandonment, neglect, abuse (physically, mentally, verbally, sexually), or enmeshment (relationship between people in which personal boundaries are permeable and unclear)—as an infant, child, or adolescent, our first feeling response is *Fear*.

Children always self-blame because of the God Principle. As previously mentioned, parents are in the position of Mr. & Mrs. God to their children, as they represent the masculine and feminine nature of our Creator. Therefore, children want to please their parents (as we wish to please God), and if their parents get upset,

SECTION ONE—TIME

LAYERS OF OUR PERSONALITY

Affection, Affirmation, Acceptance

© Richard Cohen, M.A., January 2019

the child personalizes it thinking, "God doesn't like me," or "What I did was wrong. I am bad."

Beneath psychological fear are *Guilt* and *Shame*. Guilt is associated with our belief system and behavior, "I did something wrong." Shame is associated with our being, "I am bad, flawed, unlovable." If we are allowed to express our feelings freely, and if our feelings are heard and honored by our parents and/or caregivers, healing occurs at the time of the hurt.

On the other hand, if our feelings are not expressed or received, then we repress them. "Repression is a state of emotional numbness.... It occurs when you are tired of resisting, resenting, and rejecting that you successfully repress all of your negative emotions to 'keep the peace,' for the sake of the family, or to look good to the world" (Gray, John, *What You Feel, You Can Heal*, Mill Valley, CA: Heart Publishing, 1984, page 84).

If the abandonment, neglect, abuse, or enmeshment continues, the next feeling response will be *Anger*. Anger is a physiological response to danger and a psychological response to hurt and pain. If we express our anger, and our parents allow us to do so in a constructive manner, then our painful emotions are resolved. If our parents or caregivers do not allow us to express our anger, then we repress our hurts and pain. *Feelings buried alive never die. Time alone does not heal all wounds, it just buries them deeper.*

Finally, we will develop coping skills, defensive mechanisms, and character armor to survive in an environment where our thoughts and feelings go unheard and basic love needs go unmet. These coping skills, defensive mechanisms, and character armor represent the *False Self*.

The interesting thing about these coping skills and defensive mechanisms is that they are based on our original nature, our God-given gifts, i.e. caregiver, performer, activist, etc. However, these gifts are then used for a dual purpose: 1) to mask our hurts, pain, guilt, and shame, and 2) to obtain the affection, affirmation, and acceptance never received or perceived.

The layer of the *False Self* contains the many masks we wear, the games we play, the character armor we put on, and the defensive mechanisms we use to shield our wounded heart from further hurt and pain—pleaser, perfectionist, performer, pusher, controller, self-righteous, clown, victim, etc. The problem is, no matter how hard we work to gain the affection, affirmation, and acceptance that we need, it will never soothe our souls. The reason is that such behavior is driven by a need for recognition—being loved for what we *do*, rather than for who we genuinely *are*.

•••••••••••••••••••••••••••••••••

We all possess a primal need to be accepted for who we are, not for what we do, not for how we look, and not for our accomplishments.

•••••••••••••••••••••••••••••••••

The three As listed below the layer of the False Self are Affection, Affirmation, and Acceptance. These are the normal needs of every child, adolescent, and adult. However, our False Self is using these needs in an unconscious manner, using our character armor and defensive mechanisms to obtain love: Affection (healthy physical touch), Affirmation (for our innate abilities and talents), and Acceptance (just for who we are).

I did not include Approval on the list of three As because approval is behavior-based. It is normal if a parent, partner, boss, friend, or God does not approve of our behavior(s). Behavior has to do with our doing, not our being. Therefore, we can still be loved for who we are, even if someone does not approve of our behavior (what we say or do).

If it remains unhealed, the False Self leads to another layer called *Illnesses and Disorders*. Many healers believe that most illnesses and disorders have a psychological basis, the result of unresolved relationships (negative bonding patterns), lack of physical affection, and negative attitudes and beliefs. Each part of our being affects the other—spirit, body, mind, and heart. This is why recovering and discovering our true self or inner child takes time (more about the inner child later).

We must peel away the layers of our personality one by one, like an onion. We cannot move right into the core of our being and dismantle our personality too quickly. We must remove each defensive layer systematically, and then replace each coping mechanism with healthy ways of being, thinking, and behaving.

Finally, we need to grieve the many losses of our past. The grieving process takes time. When we have gained a sufficient sense of self-worth from our relationship with God, self, and others, then we move deeper into recovering our true selves.

Exercise

Now using the Layers of Our Personality chart, put circles around every issue that you have dealt with successfully and resolved. Put rectangles around every issue that you are still dealing with at the present time. Keep this as a reference as you continue to work through your issues.

Methods of Self-Healing

Stage One:	Behavioral changes: Support network
Stage Two:	Cognitive changes: Affirmations
Stage Three:	Healing your inner child
Stage Four:	Healing opposite-sex wounds
Stage Five:	Healing same-sex wounds

SECTION ONE—TIME

Stage One: Behavioral changes

SUPPORT NETWORK

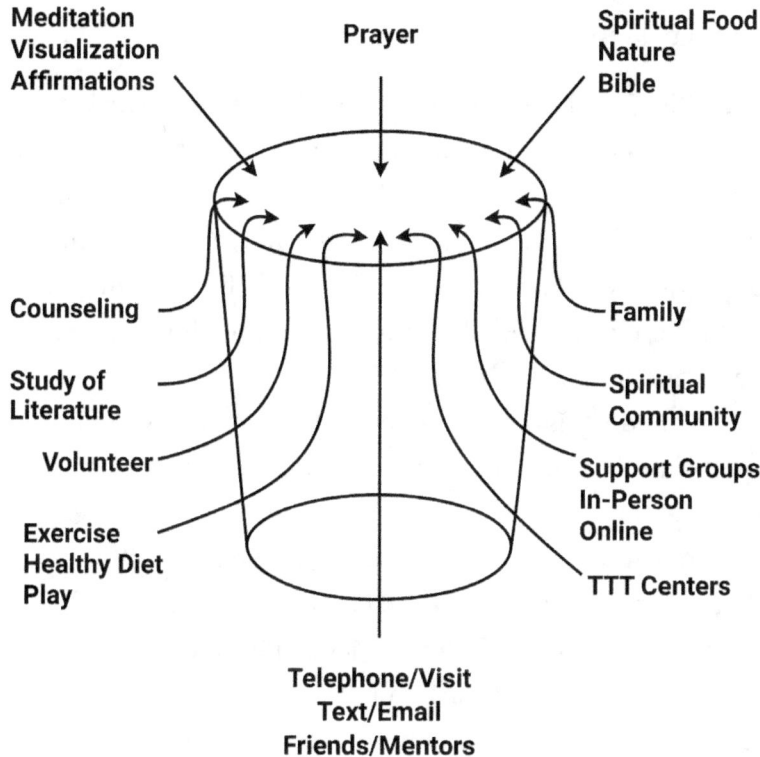

© Richard Cohen, M.A., 2019

Support Network

"It is an established fact that nobody is born with the ability to love himself. Self-love is either acquired or it is non-existent. The one who does not acquire it or who acquires it insufficiently either is not able to love others at all or to love themselves only insufficiently. The same would be true for such a person in his relationship with God. To put it bluntly, whoever does not love himself is an egoist. He must become an egoist necessarily because he is not sure of his identity and is therefore always trying to find himself" (Trobisch, Walter, *Love Yourself*, Downers Grove, IL: Intervarsity Press, 1978, pages. 8-9).

The Support Network consists of different behaviors and relationships to help us internalize love while developing a new family of choice. The container in this drawing represents each one of us. On the top of the container we receive God's love through prayer, studying His Word, creative visualization (while listening to beautiful music and positive affirmations), and spending time in Nature (the second Bible).

Surrounding us on the road of recovery are many resources and opportunities for experiencing love: family, spiritual community, support groups (in-person or online), TTT centers (to be explained in the conclusion), friends and mentors, exercise, healthy diet, play, volunteer, study of literature, and counseling (if necessary).

If you grew up in a dysfunctional family and environment, you now have the chance to change your destiny by creating a *new family of choice*. Building a strong Support Network is an essential part of your healing. It is recreating a new family of choice in a healthy, positive, loving, and supportive manner. By spending time with a loving God, who accepts you just the way you are, and listening to positive affirmations (how to create your own affirmation MP3 follows next), your inner world begins to soften and accepts being loved.

Asking your family, friends, and mentors for their support will be critical in the later stages of healing. First you must create a team who will care for you in both good and bad times. "No man is an island entire of itself; every man is a piece of the continent, a part of the main," John Donne, Meditation XVII. The components of your support network stand as a fortress of strength. This is the holding environment, the fertile soil in which you will spring forth and grow.

Today there are many in-person and online support groups. Do a simple Internet search for groups that suit your particular need, i.e., Sexaholics Anonymous, Co-Dependents Anonymous, Sex and Love Addicts Anonymous, Alcoholics Anonymous, Emotions Anonymous, Overeaters Anonymous, Narcotics Anonymous, Gamblers Anonymous, etc. You were raised in a community of people, and you need to heal in the presence of others. If your family is not safe, if you lack friends and mentors, it is time to build new relationships that foster healing and growth. Start by joining local and/or online support groups.

Find mentors in your place of worship, support group (sponsors), therapy group, Meetup group, wherever you find another person who is further along on the path of healing. Establish a regular time to meet with your mentor/sponsor, either in person or online. Consistency is essential to establish a bond of trust.

Once again: *You must be real and feel in order to heal.* By sharing your truth with another person, and not being judged for who you are and what you have done, then you will experience trust and love. These relationships will serve as a net to catch you when you need to fall apart. I guarantee that without such support, you will not be able to heal your wounds and fulfill unmet love needs. *What was created in unhealthy relationships must be healed in healthy relationships.* Start today to create your new family of choice.

Regular exercise and a healthy diet are also essential components of healing. We are what we eat—plant-based diets and natural foods nourish our bodies. For some food equals love, while for others it is the opposite and food is the enemy. Today more and more women and men are bulimic, anorexic, or overweight. All are masks to cover up low self-worth and numb our pain. Overeaters Anonymous and other groups support those who struggle with food. Will power alone will not carry you through this battle. Find those who have been through your struggle and learn from them. Find a sponsor or mentor to accompany you on your journey.

Having fun and play time is essential throughout our adulthood. Whether it's a game of tennis, basketball, soccer, swinging on the swings in a park, seeing a movie, these are just a few playful activities to help us keep our lives in balance. I will share more about fun activities in the inner child section.

Volunteering in our communities is a way to contribute to others. There is a danger during our healing activities to become too introspective. Look for opportunities in your area to help those in need. This will make you feel better while helping others. Balance healing work with playfulness and acts of service. Volunteering in your community is a wonderful source of positive energy.

There are excellent books to help you understand why you do whatever it is that you don't want to do. Learn from seasoned warriors who have fought the battles and won the wars. They will save you lots of time, unnecessary pain, and money on the journey home.

If you need counseling, find a successful and competent therapist, one who has overcome his or her own issues. Do not spend your hard-earned money on a "professional" counselor or therapist if they are not successful in their personal lives. For example, if you want marriage counseling, you need a therapist who has a beautiful relationship with his or her spouse. If you are struggling with an addiction, you need a therapist who understands your issue and has had personal success in overcoming his own battles.

Search for and find a well-trained, professionally successful, and personally victorious counselor. Ask, "How can you help me?

What is your education? What therapeutic tools do you use? How successful have you been in your practice helping people like me? What is your success rate? And finally, how is your personal life? Have you worked through your own issues? Are you married, and if so, are you happy in your marriage?" If it is important to you, please ask, "Do you believe in God? Do you bring spirituality into the therapeutic process? If so, how?"

If the therapist becomes defensive and will not answer your questions, do not waste your time with such a person. Remember, you will be sharing the deepest, darkest aspects of your soul with this man or woman. Be sure that he or she is transparent and well qualified both personally and professionally.

The more you develop a strong Support Network, the more stable and content you will become. The Support Network represents your family of choice and becomes the foundation for your healing journey.

Stage Two: Cognitive changes

Most of us develop negative thought patterns about ourselves and others as a result of temperament and experiences with family, friends, community, and social pressure during the formative years of child development. It is not an event that causes us to feel bad; it is our belief system or interpretation of the event that creates a negative response. The Greek philosopher Epictetus said, "Men are not disturbed by things, but by the view they take of them." Cognitive therapy calls this the ABC model:

- **A**ctivating Event—something happens that leads us to feel bad.
- **B**elief System—our underlying or unconscious beliefs about the event.

- <u>C</u>onsequential Feelings—our beliefs about what happened cause us to feel bad.

In David Burns excellent workbook *Ten Days to Self-Esteem* (Harper Collins, New York, 1993, 1999), he provides practical skills to turn our cognitive distortions or "stinkin' thinkin'" into positive thoughts and feelings. I suggest doing one chapter every two weeks in order to internalize all the important life skills to transform your thoughts and feelings. His most important skill is the Daily Mood Log, a simple and effective method to: 1) describe the triggering event which made you feel bad, 2) the resultant feelings, and 3) a three-column technique to list how you think about what happened, identify the negative thoughts, and develop positive responses. By practicing the Daily Mood Log on a regular basis, harmful feelings will soon be replaced with positive thoughts and emotions. Another wonderful book to resolve negative thinking is *Mind Over Mood*, 2nd edition, by Dennis Greenberger and Christine A. Padesky (Guilford Press, New York, 2016).

Did you hear the joke about the man who went to the football game? He turns to his friend and says, "I have to leave!" "Why, we just got here?" replied his friend. "Because the team is in a huddle and they're talking about me." Sounds funny, yes? But perception becomes reality. *Dealing with negative self-talk is a vital part of creating peace within.*

The new field of neuroplasticity has scientifically proven that our brain changes through repeated thought patterns and behaviors. This fantastic news means that we can change at any age or stage in our lives. Once again, please practice all the simple and effective skills in either Dr. Burns *Ten Days to Self-Esteem* or Dr. Greenberger and Padesky's *Mind Over Mood*.

Affirmations

Listening to affirmations, or positive messages, on a regular basis will also transform the way you think and feel about yourself and others.

> "Social psychologists tell us that the average person has approximately 25,000 thoughts each day. Some studies suggest that it could be as high as 72,000 a day, depending on how one defines a thought. Perhaps of most significance is that as many as 90-95 percent of those thoughts are the same ones we think repeatedly day after day ... Such negative thoughts as fear make us anxious or angry and cause adrenaline to surge in our bodies. Powerless and critical thoughts bring depression by changing the serotonin level in our brains ... Even our brain chemistry is changed immediately in response to each of our thoughts and the feelings that follow. As long as we think the thoughts we have always thought, with the frequency with which we have thought them, and as unconsciously, our lives and our relationships can never consistently improve, for we will be imprisoned in the ego mind's way of thinking. Until we become the master of our minds, we cannot take charge of our feelings or our relationships, and we will experience ourselves as being at the effect of others—essentially an experience of victimization" (Grayson, Henry, *Mindful Loving*, New York: Penguin Publishing Group, 2003, pages 67-70).

•••••••••••••••••••••••••••••••••••••••

Shockingly, 70-80% of our repeated daily thoughts are negative.

•••••••••••••••••••••••••••••••••••••••

(Raghunathan, R.(2013, October 10), How Negative is Your "Mental Chatter"?, *Psychology Today*, https://www.psychologytoday.com/us/blog/sapient-nature/201310/how-negative-is-your-mental-chatter) and (Galloza, Stephen (2012, March 22) 80% of Thoughts are Negative... 95% are Repetitive, https://faithhopeandpsychology.wordpress.com/2012/03/02/80-of-thoughts-are-negative-95-are-repetitive/.)

By listening to your personalized affirmations, you will begin to change the neural pathways in your brain and improve your overall sense of self-worth. Affirmations help quiet your inner critic while improving your overall health and wellbeing.

Exercise

Please make two lists:
1. Things that you wish your mom and/or dad had said to you, and things that you wish they had done with you while you were growing up; and
2. Things that you wish your siblings and/or peers had said to you, and things that you wish they had done with you while you were growing up.

Make sure that each sentence is in the present tense with only positive words and phrases. There should be no words such as "not," "won't," "can't," and "shouldn't" in the affirmations. For example, do not say "You aren't stupid." It should be turned into a positive sentiment. So, if you're not stupid, then what are you? Smart! Reframe it and say, "You are smart." The reason that we omit negative words is because our unconscious, or inner child, will omit the modifier and only hear, "You are stupid."

After completing your lists, choose people that you trust to represent your parents, siblings, and/or peers (if your parents and siblings have either passed away, are unavailable, or are unwilling). Your chosen people will record the affirmations. It is of the utmost importance that the persons who record this MP3 (or whatever format you chose) share from their hearts, not just their heads. It must impact your soul, your inner child. Also, have them leave a space of equal time after each sentence so that you may repeat it in your mind, making it more personal. For example, they will say, "I love you just the way you are." Then, in that time of silence after they speak, you say to yourself, "You love me just the way I am," or "I am loved just the way I am." Say this silently in your mind, to your heart.

After making the recording, put beautiful music in the background, which helps your heart to heal while listening to these wonderful words of affirmation. The finished recording generally lasts about 5-10 minutes. Ideally listen upon waking in the morning and before going to bed at night. If that is too much at first, then start with a small dosage, perhaps listening to the affirmations several times per week, and then systematically increase the dosage until you are listening twice daily. I promise that if you listen to these affirmations for a minimum of three to four months, it will begin to transform your sense of self-worth and wellbeing. It is advisable to listen to your affirmations for one year. Again, neuroplasticity assures us that the brain changes: *Neurons that fire together wire together. Neurons that fire apart, wires depart.*

Now, an interesting phenomenon will occur when you start listening to your affirmations. At first it may be wonderful to hear the words you always longed to hear from your loved ones and friends. But then you may begin to get very angry or negative: "Why now? Why not then? Why do you say you love me now? I don't believe you." Please be assured that these are normal and healthy reactions. If this occurs, press pause and then express all your negative thoughts and feelings. Scream, cry, get angry, and let it out. The more you release, the quicker you heal. Once you have finished releasing the hurtful thoughts and feelings, press play and listen once again until you need to further detox. Keep repeating this process until you empty your emotional bucket. It takes time. It took years to create those wounds, so they won't disappear overnight. Give yourself grace and time to heal, and let the love penetrate deep into your soul.

Below is an example of affirmations from a previous client:

Positive messages from father to son:

- I love you son.
- I want to spend time with you.
- I am proud to be your father.
- I appreciate you.
- You are handsome.
- You are very important to me.
- I love you son, and I give you my blessing.
- You are talented and smart.
- You are strong, brave, and courageous.
- I love you just the way you are.
- You exceed my expectations as a son.

Positive messages from peers:

- We are your friends, and we admire you.
- You belong.
- We accept you.
- You are strong and powerful.
- We want to hang out with you.
- We look up to you.
- We enjoy being around you.
- You deserve the best.
- I'd pick you first to be on my team.
- We appreciate you.
- I like to be buddies with you.
- We love you.

Stage Three: Healing your inner child

When we go from infancy to old age,
our inner children are always present in our lives and heart.
When we become old, we become as a child once again.

© Richard Cohen, M.A., 2019

The concept of Inner Child was developed by Carl Jung, Emmet Fox, Charles Whitefield, Alice Miller, and other professional therapists. It is a marvelous understanding about getting in touch with your unconscious—the precious little boy or girl that lives within your heart. Learn to listen to that voice within. He or she is your best teacher in matters of the heart, and what matters most in your life. Of course, your adult or higher self remains in the position of CEO to your inner family.

The most excellent workbook to assist you on this journey is *Recovery of Your Inner Child* by Dr. Lucia Capacchione. The exercises will help you discover a whole new world. Although it may seem ridiculous at times, please continue. The book is full of wisdom to unlock the treasures of your heart. The eleven chapters deal with discovering your inner child, exploring your inner parents, and getting in touch with your magical, playful, and spiritual inner child.

Seven Stages of Development

Stage	Time	Activity	Needs	Learns
Bonding	0-6/9 months	Cries	Mirroring	Being Trust Hope
Exploring	0-6/9 months 18/24months	Explores	Protection	Doing Self-Motivation Will
Separation	18/24 months -3 years	Rebels	Acceptance/ Limits	Thinking Independence Will
Socialization	3-5/6 years	Questions	Answers	Identity Power Purpose Cause-Effect
Latency	5/6- 12/13 years	Doing Arguing	Rules Reasons	Skills Structure Negotiation Competence
Adolescence	12/13- 18/21 years	All of the above in a more mature form		Identity Sexuality Separation Autonomy
Adulthood	18/21 years- rest of life	Recycle through all stages in ways that support specific adult tasks		Independence Interdependence Fidelity

Source: Jon and Laurie Weiss, *Recovery from Codependency*, used by permission from the authors.

SECTION ONE—TIME

This wonderful chart describes the ages and stages of development that you went through from childhood to adulthood. If you got stuck at any stage of growth because of unhealed wounds or unmet love needs, that part of your heart and mind still remains frozen in time. You must go back and reawaken your child within.

Each of us has a wounded and vulnerable inner child. The inner child is simply another name for your original or true self. Due to the slings and arrows of outrageous fortune you may have suffered while growing up, you then built walls around your heart to survive the hurt and pain. Your Golden Child, pure self, may have learned to hide behind the castle walls, thick walls around your hidden heart, afraid to let someone in, to truly know you.

Each one of us may have developed different facades to protect and guard us, as we peer out through various shaped windows, so that others may only see a part of us, while we, defensively, can see them. We may think that we see them, however, we most likely are

Everyone is looking out of their windows at each other, protecting their hearts.

©Richard Cohen, M.A., 2019

only viewing the small parts (sub-personalities) they show us, as they peek out of their own tiny windows from behind their wall! Most of us are so afraid to let others in, and so afraid to be seen.

Once again, *you must feel and be real in order to heal.* You need to implement a program to recover and discover your beautiful child within. Then you will move from victim to victor.

So many of us live in Victimland and speak Victimese. By discovering and recovering your child within, you will become a Victor of Love, taking back your power that was lost in childhood and/or adolescence. What you cannot accept in others is a reflection of your own shadow, lost part, frozen child, or dormant part. Popular rapper Eminem, known for his defiant and angry music and lyrics, may be expressing our own repressed rage. His song Venom opens with the words, "I got a song filled with shit for the strong willed. When the world gives you a raw deal. Set you off 'til you scream, 'Piss off, screw you!'" We create terrorists and murderers by denying our own anger and rage. When we express our anger and pain in healthy ways, when we get in touch with our inner child, we heal the world a bit more of Pain Pollution.

Discovering My Inner Child

When I first discovered my inner child, it was like having my sight restored after being blind since childhood! Suddenly I was able to experience all the senses: touch, smell, sight, sound, and taste came alive. I was overwhelmed by colors, dimensions, nuances that seem almost unreal. Getting back in touch with my inner child was an amazing experience. Sometimes the journey was messy, and at other times it seemed as if I entered a parallel universe.

Getting back in touch with my inner child started one day when I was looking at photos of my childhood. I saw a beautiful, happy, extroverted, confident, bubbly two-year old and thought, "Who is that? What happened to her? Where did she go?" As I investigated old photo albums, it became clear that at a certain age not long after those photos were taken, that bubbly child had disappeared. Where had she gone? Where was the two-year old who marched into restaurants, walked up to people's tables to say hello, sneaked out of the house and ran down the street to the bus stop because she wanted to visit her daddy's office in the city center. What turned those sparkling eyes into pits of sadness, those inquisitive eyes into blank empty holes?

I am an artist and visual woman, so my "picture" of what happened is as follows: In my childhood home, one by one, my vulnerable, creative, joyful, wise inner children got sent to bed without dinner in a dark room, because I had replied incorrectly. Another part of my inner family was sent into a beautiful room to hide and protect herself when my parents were arguing violently. Part of my character was relegated to a huge cryotherapy room to freeze the shame of when she was abused. And, finally, a beautiful part of my soul was taken to a beautiful land of God to survive the emotional and physical devastation of abuse, not only experienced as a victim but as a bystander as well. This is how I coped with the insanity of my early years.

Discovering my inner family has meant walking through my childhood home and knocking on each door to reacquaint myself with different parts of my heart. I had to earn the trust of my inner children. Those who had been "punished" were terrified of being seen or even existing. Those who were happy had no intention of leaving their peaceful and perfect parallel universe. I had to mediate with protectors who had the job of keeping my inner children safe. As an adult, I created a mature, emotional ego-structure to welcome my inner family. And, most important, I had to deal with a hyper-critical inner parent. This was a daunting task. To counter the critic, I developed a nurturing and loving inner parent who embraced my inner children—rebellious child, angry child, playful child, and creative child.

I know, it sounds like madness and sometimes that's what it feels like, but I have learned that true reality is more beautiful than I dared to imagine. It was like having a video of my life at certain times when the frame got stuck and frozen. Now I have had the opportunity to replay certain parts, restore and recover my precious inner family. No longer frozen, I am becoming freed.

—Chantal

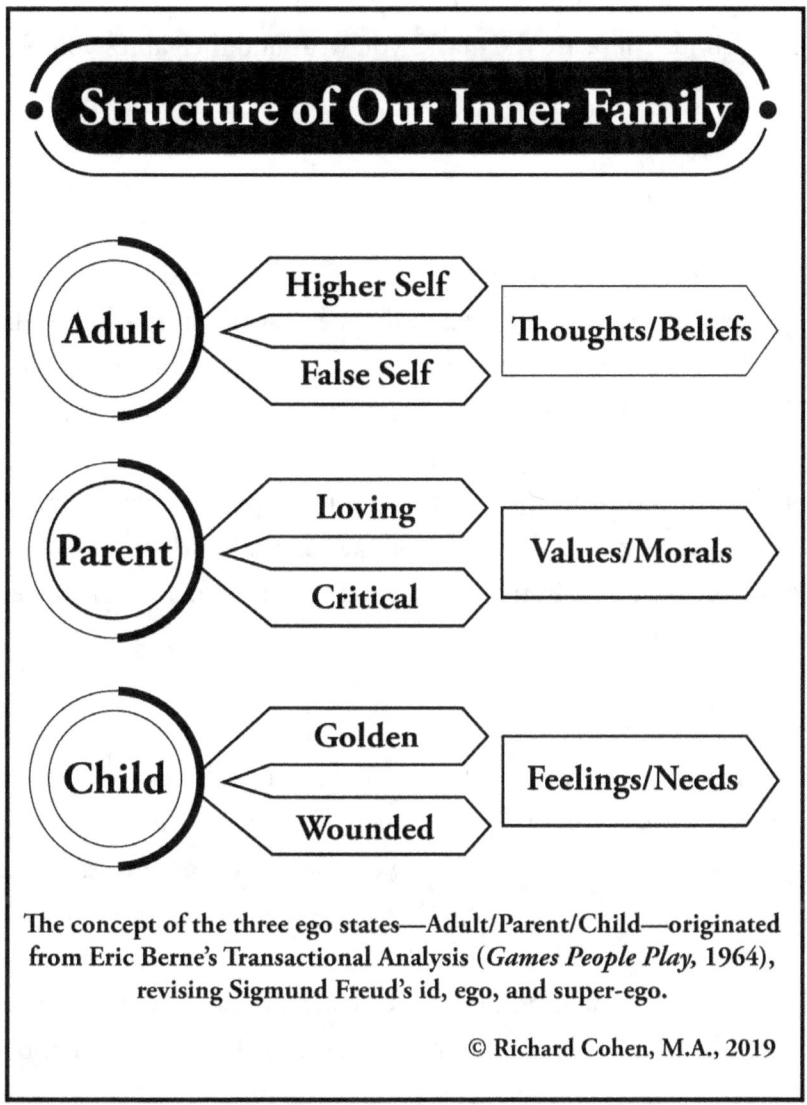

The concept of the three ego states—Adult/Parent/Child—originated from Eric Berne's Transactional Analysis (*Games People Play*, 1964), revising Sigmund Freud's id, ego, and super-ego.

© Richard Cohen, M.A., 2019

Adult

This is your higher self, or true self, with understanding, problem-solving abilities, unconditional love, forgiveness, connectedness, and a strong sense of self-worth. The shadow side, or dark side, is the false self, the protective armor, character defenses, coping strategies that you developed to protect your wounded inner child. These are the masks you wear and the games you play to shield yourself from further pain. The adult focuses on thoughts and beliefs.

Parent

There is the healthy, loving, nurturing, and protecting inner parent that affirms, appreciates, and accepts your inner child. The healthy parent uplifts, encourages, and praises your inner child. The shadow side, or dark side, is the critical, unloving inner parent who may be either judgmental, critical, cold, conditional, abusive, or neglectful of your inner child. The inner parental voices are an accumulation of introjections from parents, authority figures, religious figures, and cultural messages. The parent focuses on values, ethics, and morals.

Inner Child

You have a healthy, authentic, genuine, or true inner child full of wonder, love, creativity, playfulness, magical thinking, and true spirituality. The shadow side is your wounded or broken inner child, who may experience either pain, heartaches, guilt, shame, loneliness, fear, despair, hopelessness, and/or misperceptions. Your wounded inner child may be an accumulation of your unresolved heartaches, your parents' unresolved issues, and/or those inherited from previous generations. The inner child focuses on feelings and needs.

To change your life in the present, you need to awaken, discover, recover, and heal the wounded child and children within, i.e., angry child, hurt child, frightened child. You need to bring into consciousness that which has remained unconscious. You need to quiet the voice of your inner critical parent, and develop a loving, encouraging, nurturing, and protecting inner parent. Unless you bring into the light that which has been in the darkness, those parts of you will continuously sabotage all adult efforts to succeed and will create "dis-ease" in your present life. Therefore, you need to heal the unresolved wounds of your past.

Three Steps to Heal Your Inner Child

Self-Parenting

- Listen to your thoughts, feelings, and needs.
- Be a good parent to your inner child through time, touch, and talk.
- Create healing activities.

Spiritual Parenting

- Prayer, meditation, and study.
- Experience value as a daughter or son of God.
- Healing of memories with spiritual mentors.

Mentoring or Re-parenting

- Heal hetero-emotional and/or homo-emotional wounds.
- Experience love through mentoring relationships.
- Participate in healing activities.

© Richard Cohen, M.A. 2019

To begin this process of healing, first listen to the voices of your inner family. Then you will learn to distinguish who is speaking and ascertain how to satisfy the needs of your inner child in healthy and appropriate ways. You may also need to discipline and set boundaries for your inner brat or inner tyrant who wants his way, the way he wants it, when he wants it.

Martha Baldwin describes this character as the Saboteur. "Ignoring the Saboteur empowers it. Trying to get rid of it only teaches it to hide itself in more clever ways. The only route to ending self-sabotage is through facing and knowing the Saboteur intimately. Only then can you acknowledge its destructiveness, accept its presence, learn to contain its power, and say 'no' to its attempts to destroy your life. Only when you ignore and deny its existence can the Saboteur do its deadly work secretly and successfully" (Baldwin, Martha, *Self-Sabotage*, New York, Warner Books, 1987, page 23).

Step One: Self-Parenting

1. Listen to your thoughts, feelings, and needs
2. Be a good parent to your inner child: time, touch, and talk
3. Create healing activities

First, learn to listen to the voice of your inner child by doing the exercises in *Recovery of Your Inner Child,* by Dr. Lucia Capacchione. Before you look to others to take care of your needs, you must first become a good parent to yourself. You need to enhance and/or create a nurturing inner parent and quiet the critic. Most of us desperately want acceptance. First, you must learn to accept yourself before looking to others for acceptance. Otherwise, others determine your wellbeing by how they think and feel about you, rather than how you think and feel about yourself. World peace begins within us, not outside of ourselves.

By doing the exercises in *Recovery of Your Inner Child*, you will learn to identify the different parts of your inner family—the vulnerable child, angry child, nurturing parent, protective parent, critical parent, wounded child, playful, creative, and spiritual children. It is an excellent primer to begin inner-child recovery. You will need a sketch pad and colored pencils and/or crayons. Please do the drawing and writing exercises, one chapter every two weeks (slower or quicker if you wish). It is important to complete all the assignments. It will be of tremendous benefit for your life, and the life of your family. (By the way, I have done all the exercises in *Recovery of Your Inner Child* at least eight times over the past twenty years. Each time I re-read the book and do the exercises, I learn more about my inner family. It's a most excellent tool for personal growth and development. My wife and our children have also done the exercises in this book. It was wonderful sharing our homework together as a family.)

Second, spend time with your inner child, e.g., drawing, dialogue, meditation. John Pollard's book, *Self-Parenting: The Complete Guide to Your Inner Conversations*, describes a simple and effective method to dialogue with your inner child. Get a notebook and draw a line down the center of each page. On the left side, with your dominant hand, allow the voice of your inner parent to speak. On the right side, with your nondominant hand, allow the voice of your inner child to speak. In this way, both voices communicate and share with each other.

It may sound bizarre and strange, but it really works and is very therapeutic. The reason to draw or write with your nondominant hand is that it bypasses the intellectual neurology and gets you in touch with your body and emotions. The left hemisphere of your brain is the more analytical, intellectual, logical, and verbal. The right hemisphere is more emotional, artistic, and intuitive. Even if you are left handed, as I am, using nondominant hand drawing and writing works beautifully.

Meditation is another tool to access your inner child. I have developed several Inner Child (MP3) meditations (https://sellfy.com/p/VWIK/). While doing the exercises from Capacchione's book, I suggest using the inner child meditations simultaneously (two or three times per week). You may also check online for other wonderful inner child meditations.

Third, create healing activities for your inner child, i.e., bike rides, walks in the park, skating, dancing, eating ice cream, swinging on swings, taking a trip. Through dialogue, drawing, and meditation, your inner child will reveal what he or she needs. It is important to meet those needs in a timely and appropriate manner. Most important: Never make promises that you don't intend to keep. It would be like promising your own child that you will do something with him or her, and not following through. Consistency is key to successful parenting. You must keep your word. In this way, your inner child will begin to trust you, and then reveal increasingly deeper truths.

Step Two: Spiritual Parenting

1. Prayer, meditation, and study
2. Experience value as a son or daughter of God
3. Healing of memories with spiritual mentors

First, through prayer, meditation, and study, you may access several wounds and needs of your inner child/children. Second, use your affirmation recording to restore your inner child's sense of self-worth. The important thing is to continuously infuse your mind, heart, and spirit, experiencing your value as a precious child of God.

"Affirmations are basically a form of auto-suggestion, and when practiced deliberately and repeatedly, they reinforce chemical pathways in the brain, strengthening neural connections. Says David J. Hellerstein, M.D., a Professor of Clinical Psychiatry at Columbia University, 'In brief, we have realized that "neuroplasticity," the ongoing remodeling of brain structure and function, occurs throughout life. It can be affected by life experiences, genes, biological agents, and by behavior, as well as by thought patterns.' Neuroscience now proves that our thoughts can change the structure and function of our brains. By practicing positive thought patterns (affirmations) repetitively, we actually create neuroplasticity in the area of the brain that processes what we are thinking about. The key is repetition so you flood your brain with the positive thought" (https://liveboldandbloom.com/08/quotes/positive-affirmations).

The third task of Step Two is the use of memory healing. Through creative visualization—the art of using mental imagery and affirmations to produce positive changes in your life—you may help your inner child access painful memories and while there imagine being protected, loved, and mentored. A spiritual mentor may be a religious figure (Christ, David, Mary, etc.), an idealized parent, a trusted friend, a loved one, or one's own parent(s) in an idealized form. During your visualizations, you may invite your spiritual mentor into the room, or sacred space, to show you love and/or perhaps rescue you from someone who caused you harm in childhood. You may also use the Inner Child meditations to help you visualize the transformation of past memories into positive experiences of love with the assistance of your spiritual mentor(s).

If you are ready to retrieve and release hurts from your past, this is a very effective tool for healing. Please note that if the memory is one of severe trauma, you must heal those wounds in the presence of a "sympathetic witness," someone to be there through the pain and process of healing, and perhaps to hold you if necessary. Again and again: *What was created in unhealthy relationships must be healed in healthy relationships.*

Memory healing may also be used to create wonderful and happy experiences. The spiritual mentor may engage with your inner child in fun, learning, and nurturing activities, thus fulfilling your deepest unmet needs. Through creative visualizations, the spiritual mentor may play ball, go fishing, take a walk, or hold your inner child.

Stage Three: Mentoring

1. Healing past wounds
2. Mentoring or re-parenting relationships
3. Creating friendships and activities

First, after you have gained a greater sense of self-worth, self-knowledge, and self-parenting skills, reach out and have others assist in the process of healing relationship wounds. The first and best choice are your parents. If your parent or parents are available, capable, and willing, excellent. However if they are unwilling, deceased, or unhealthy, then find supportive, loving men and women who can act as "Second Chance Parents" (Jarema, William J., *Fathering the Next Generation*, Crossroad, 1995).

Second, if you belong to a church, synagogue, mosque, or spiritual organization, it is natural to seek mentors from your faith community. The point is to find mentors who act as the loving and supportive mom and/or dad that you never experienced. Successfully married men and women make excellent mentors. A few roles of the mentor may be: 1) offer unconditional love, 2) speak words of affirmation, 3) teach about healthy boundaries in relationships and basic life skills, 4) participate in shared activities, 5) pray for the adult-child, and 6) offer the gift of healthy touch.

Some of the roles of the adult-child may be: 1) express needs in healthy ways, 2) work through stages of dependency-independence-interdependence, 3) break through defensive barriers—resistance to open up and allow yourself to be loved, 4) learn new social skills, and 5) forgive those who hurt you.

> "When you long for something, it becomes a source of pain. Therefore, getting what you want is painful. We're not prepared for that. If I long to be touched and I hunger to be touched, I will actually resist your (someone) touching me.
>
> "For years, I longed to be touched. I knew I was touch-deprived. From an early age, I didn't get enough touching . . . so I came into adulthood with this need for touching, this longing for touch. But there was also a resistance to touch because getting what you want is painful. You have to have the maturity to live through the pain, that bittersweet experience of getting what you want.
>
> "Touching is so elementary to our existence. If you don't get touched when you are an infant, you die. It's not an option. You have to have tactile stimulation to survive. As an adult, you don't need it to survive, but you need it to thrive. It is such an important element to be touched that when you get touched, you often get in touch with the grief experience of not having it. That's the way it is with anything you've longed for" (Love, Patricia, *Hot Monogamy*, Sounds True Audio Tapes, No. 2, Side A. 1994; also from her book of the same title, 2012, pages 263-264).

You may heal wounds and fulfill unmet needs in the context of such a loving, mentoring relationship. I envision the elders of our communities, whose children have grown up and left home, being wonderful mentors for those of us who desperately need parenting (more about this in the next section on Touch). It is a win-win situation for all involved. The young receive blessing from the elders, and the elders receive their rightful position in our culture, being respected for their wisdom and love.

Third, it is very important to hang out and have fun with friends. This, too, provides opportunities for healing. If you do not have friends, attend groups where you will find like-minded men and women. Stretch yourself, move out of your comfort zone. *Isolation equals death!* We exist in relationships.

One final note: I have learned over the past thirty years as a psychotherapist, and through my own personal healing, to distinguish the voices of my inner child, body, and soul. The soul is a combination of your heart (inner child), mind (adult), and will (parent). When becoming acquainted with your inner child, please realize that your body and/or other parts of your soul may also be sharing.

Stage Four: Healing Opposite-Sex Wounds

In this stage of healing you will address opposite sex wounds: father-daughter, mother-son, and wounding that occurred with opposite sex family members or friends. Once again: *Feelings buried alive never die*, and *we must feel and be real in order to heal.*

This process will look different for each person because our wounds and unmet love needs are unique. But the principles of healing are the same:

1. **Recall the events or experiences** that created your opposite-sex wounds.
2. **Revisit the wounds**, together with a sympathetic witness. You cannot work through your core pain alone.

3. **Release the hurt** in your heart. Grieving may consist of tears, rage, anger, laughter, and other emotions. *If you can feel it, then you can heal it.* Without moving through your emotions and feelings, the defensive blocks will remain in place and healing will not occur. *Unwanted behaviors are connected to your unresolved wounds and unmet love needs.* When the walls come down, then love comes in, and you will experience a new sense of freedom.

4. **Realize the truth.** While grieving, have your mentor ask you, "What did you come to believe about yourself and others as a result of this experience?" Then listen to your heart and head. "You will KNOW the truth, and the truth will make you free" (John 8:32). Underneath your wounds are core beliefs that created imprints in your mind, social constructs about relationships that have negatively and unconsciously mapped the trajectory of your path in life. Some of these beliefs may be: "I don't trust men." "I don't trust women." "I am not safe." "People always leave me."

5. **Resentments be gone!** After grieving and discovering your core beliefs, it may be easier to forgive the one who hurt you, seeing the brokenness of his or her soul. Lack of forgiveness keeps you chained to the perpetrator. Therefore, forgiveness is actually the best gift you can give yourself. When you hold onto your bitterness and resentment, you will project those feelings onto others, especially those closest to you. If you cannot forgive, you may harbor unconscious guilt. Beneath the blame may be guilt and shame, the voice of your inner child, "It's all my fault."

6. **Real love** is the best medicine to restore the "years the locusts have eaten" (Joel 2:25), the years of hurt and pain taken away as a result of the original wounding. Find friends

and mentors to support you on your journey of healing, second chance fathers, mothers, brothers, and sisters.

7. **Renew your mind.** Learn new behaviors, make new choices: action, practice, action, practice. Choose new and positive core beliefs, create a new map for your life. "I trust myself." "I decide to love and be loved." Learning new patterns of thinking and behavior takes time and practice. Letting love into your heart may be scary. Breathe. Receive. Give. Breathe. Receive. Give.

> ### Finding my mother's love
>
> My mother sat on the sofa in our home. I had asked her to come over, as I needed to share something very important. My wife and friend were in the room with us. "Mom, it was very scary for me as a child to be close with you. Even though I am a man and father of two children, it's time to resolve that fear. May I please sit on your lap as I grieve the losses of my past?" "Of course," she replied.
>
> As I laid my head on my mother's breast, memories of dread and fear came flooding back. Immediately I began to cry, "Mom, it was terrorizing for me to listen to your pain about dad while growing up..." Then she interrupted and began to justify her behavior.
>
> I stood up and shouted, "Mom, please, would you just listen! I need to be heard. You don't need to respond, to explain, to do anything but hold me close and let me express all the hurt and pain lodged deep in my heart and soul. This is not about you, it's about me and how I experienced growing up." She said OK.

> Once again I sat on her lap with my head on her breast. Tears began to stream down my face. "When dad was screaming at us, and you held me close to you, all of your pain poured into my soul. I was more in pain by your pain than afraid of dad! I didn't feel safe with you, in fact, I felt like I had to take care of your needs, instead of you taking care of mine."
>
> Then I started to see pictures in my mind of my brothers physically abusing me. I started to uncontrollably cry. "Why didn't you protect me from them? Where were you? How could you let this happen?" Tears turned into rivers streaming down my face onto her blouse. She too began to cry.
>
> After grieving and releasing years of pent up pain, I felt a tremendous sense of relief. Then I said, "Mom, would you please just rub my back? It was always scary for me to feel your touch in a safe way." I took my shirt off and my mother rubbed my back. For the first time in my life, or as long as I could remember, I allowed myself to receive her motherly, loving touch. It was a turning point in my life.
>
> —John

Let me repeat this one more time: *The best gift you can give your partner and children is to heal yourself. Otherwise you pass on to the next generation all the unresolved issues of your past. Leave a legacy of real love for your children and grandchildren by healing yourself.*

If you blame your partner for your problems, remember, when you point one finger at the other person, three fingers are pointing back at you!

When you point one finger at another person, three fingers are pointing back at you!
©Richard Cohen, M.A., 2019

I had a good childhood, at least I thought I did!

"I had such a great childhood. I grew up in ideal circumstances. I am fine, just unhappy in my marriage," were the first words to my therapist. Why was he asking me all these questions about my upbringing? My parents were wonderful people. I didn't experience any physical or sexual abuse. The neighborhood in my small Catholic community was safe and secure. I had a great childhood. So what could have been so damaging that would lead me to counseling other than my marriage? Little did I know!

I had never heard of divorce or the need for therapy in our immediate circle of friends. Therefore, I felt justified to continue my defensive speech: "I had hard working parents who raised us with love, discipline, and strong values.

They were kind to us and everybody in our community, leading the senior citizen club in town for twenty-five years." Beyond that my brothers had been altar boys and Boy Scouts. I was active in the Catholic youth group and with the help of my mother, founded the Girl Scouts in our small town. The harshness and emotional distance of my grandmother towards my mother made her always watch out for my emotional needs as a girl and make efforts to stay connected to me. I felt safe with her. I felt spoiled and loved by my father, who bought me black shiny shoes with bows on them!

Still mom had no clue how to protect me from my older brothers' comments, "You are just a dumb little girl." When I was hurt by my friends she said, "Let it go, some people are just like that; they want to put others down to feel better about themselves. God knows who you are, and all will be well in heaven." Nobody had a clue that I was the overly sensitive child and needed to be listened to while processing my feelings. I shut down, acted shy and began to study people's behavior.

No one knew what was really going on within me other than my mother, who had love for me, but she couldn't help me get my voice back. I had several close girlfriends. Many of the neighborhood kids came to our house enjoying the big backyard, setting up tents, having sleep overs, and playing sports. I was not lonely on the outside, however I always had a sense of not belonging since the time I was in my mother's womb (a profound lesson that I learned later in therapy). The constant sense of not belonging, and not fitting in, did not disappear by being chosen by the school to tutor new students who needed help with their homework. The same thing happened when I became a student of fashion design. Again, I was chosen to tutor students in French and math. I knew what it felt like to have potential and not be able to reach it alone. No wonder I said what I said to the therapist, since I was completely unaware of the impact the negative imprints of my childhood had upon my life.

I tried to plant and enjoy the flowers in my emotional garden, not knowing that the roots of the weeds from the past could take over any moment. That came into play when I started dating. How come I chose the guy who turned out to be an alcoholic when things got tough? In the next relationships I was not enough—not smart enough, not sexy enough, not wealthy enough. At the age of nineteen, my heart was so crushed that I promised myself (unconsciously) to marry a sensitive, kind man who would not put me down, tell me that I was dumb, and would really see me for who I was. I fell in love at first sight with a man who loved God, was sensitive, kind and smart. He got up in the middle of the night and helped with our crying babies, cooking, and household chores. No complaint! All my girlfriends envied me.

Obviously, the universe ignored my request for my spouse to see me for who I was, or so I thought! Painfully, I discovered that I was the one who needed to look in the mirror and get therapy, digging deep down for the roots of my own doubts and insecurities. My healing journey began several years into the marriage and three thousand miles away from home. I got on my knees and prayed in my despair. Soon a new world of psychology and self-awareness opened up when I met Richard. I could not read enough self-help books, attend healing seminars, but most important was the friendship and acceptance of others. Every Wednesday evening thirty people met in my house for a support group, facilitated by Richard. This began my journey of deep emotional processing work. We were there for each other, no matter if we needed to share, to be held by somebody in the group, or make other requests for TTT. We all bonded and gained hope. We grew fast and in a safe environment.

Richard and Russell (a man in the group who was assisting Richard) became the brothers I never had. They loved me, encouraged me, saw me for who I was, and listened hours and hours to my thoughts and feelings. I received Time, Touch & Talk and it was safe, since the rule was to meet in groups of three or more. That way the wounded inner child was protected, not to be re-wounded. Each of them had different qualities to help fulfill my unmet needs for love.

It was life-changing to be held while I spoke and cried about my hurts and losses. I had mentioned that I was an unwanted child and the sensation of not belonging consumed me as early as the time in the womb. I was teased frequently by my brothers, and those negative feelings created a deep-seated sadness in my psyche. On top of that, my father withdrew from our relationship around the time I reached adolescence. He was very old-fashioned, shy, and worried to be too close to his teenage daughter who developed into a beautiful young woman. I thought I was his princess. We had done so many fun things together. What happened? What was wrong with me?

Close to forty, when I started my personal healing work, I learned to say to my inner child, "It's not your fault. The people who hurt you were already hurting because of their own life. They didn't really know who they were themselves. They did not mean to hurt you; they were victims before they ever treated you poorly. Sadly, you believed it, and therefore I will take care of parenting you now, teach you the truth about yourself from now on. You and I will take risks. I will protect you."

Nothing could stop me. I saw the light at the end of the tunnel. I had hope. I learned to nourish the relationship between my adult self (higher self), my inner parent, as well as my wounded self (inner child). All together I would say I learned to orchestrate what my soul needed for healing. Whatever I could not get from the group or my new healing partners, I created with friends who knew my value and gained an understanding of my deep personal work. They were willing to give me what I had been looking for, for so long.

Sadly, we were not taught this important understanding earlier in our lives, at home or at school, at church, or through our communities. My life changed the day I met Richard and his work. I became the woman that I wanted to be in order to save my marriage, parent my children better, and be a shining light in the world. I strongly believe that all humanity needs this kind of deeper healing to create peace on earth and achieve our full potential as children of God.

—Hilde

Here is a list of several therapeutic techniques that may facilitate the healing of core wounds. Do not be alarmed! I am not telling you to read all these books. I mention these particular techniques because they escalate healing:

Voice Dialogue (*Embracing OurSelves*, Hal & Sidra Stone)
Focusing (*Focusing*, Eugene Gendlin)
Gestalt Therapy (*Gestalt Therapy Verbatim*, Frederick Perls)
Psychodrama (*The Drama Within*, Tian Dayton)
EMDR (*Eye Movement Desensitization and Reprocessing*, Francine Shapiro)
Inner-Child Healing (*Recovery of Your Inner Child*, Lucia Chapacchine)
Family Healing Sessions (*Holding Time*, Martha Welch)
Transactional Analysis (*Games People Play*, Eric Berne)
Bioenergetics (*Bioenergetics*, Alexander Lowen / *Core Energetics*, Pierrakos)

I reference these excellent, scientifically-proven therapeutic modalities so you may ask prospective therapists about their training and expertise. Ideally, try to work with a therapist who is eclectic and educated in body-centered therapies.

"Body-Centered Psychotherapy describes therapeutic approaches that integrate a client's physical body into the therapy process. Also referred to as Somatic Psychotherapy, this is a process that recognizes the intimate relationship between the human body and the psychological wellbeing of a person. Body-Centered Psychotherapists view the body as a resource for self-discovery and healing" (http://www.ashleyeder.com/approaches/body-centered-psychotherapy/).

Principles of healing: You can only take a person as far as you have gone yourself. You cannot give what you don't have or have not experienced. That is why many therapists are not worth their weight in salt, because they have not done their own healing work. By the same token, a spouse wanting a deeper relationship with her mate, must first face her own issues, before getting closer with her partner. Parents, the same principle holds true with your children. If you want your children to heal, heal thyself first.

Many forms of couples' therapy do not work because of the blame game. First, we must heal ourselves before expecting any lasting change in our relationship. It only takes one person to change the family system. When you change, this will impact your partner and children. Think of the mobile on the side of a crib. When you touch one figure, they all move.

When you move one piece, all the other pieces move. It only takes one person in the family to change the system.

©Richard Cohen, M.A., 2019

The present is perfect, no matter how painful it may be. There is always something for us to learn. Perception is everything. God won't give you more that you can handle. That which doesn't kill you, may heal you and teach you if you allow it. Love is the ultimate message and lesson in every situation.

What you resist persists. Embrace your inner demons, those pesky unresolved issues that keep rearing their ugly heads, i.e. resentment towards those who hurt you, unwanted sexual behaviors, bitterness towards your spouse, anger issues, addictions, etc. **The path to healing goes straight through hell.** Let's say it together now: *We must be real and feel in order to heal.* There are no shortcuts in matters of the heart.

The path to healing goes through your heart, not around or over it. "A hero is no braver than the ordinary man, but he is braver five minutes longer," said Ralph Waldo Emerson. The great person makes more mistakes and keeps getting up and trying one more time. "Never, never, never give up," stated Winston Churchill. Crises are messages from your soul to STOP, reflect, and change course of being and behaving. Breakdown precedes breakthrough, death before resurrection.

There was a fork in the road, where and when you split off from your heart and developed masks to survive and cope (Layers of Our Personality: False Self). In healing, you will need to peel away the layers around your heart to restore and recover your childlike nature. One more time: *What you experienced in hurtful relationships must be healed in healthy and loving relationships.*

I guarantee that you will not heal while crying alone into your pillow at night. God does not want you to simply heal with Him. If your father left you, abused you (physically, emotionally, mentally, and/or sexually), ignored you, or otherwise treated you unkindly, then you must, *you must* find male mentors to demonstrate healthy paternal love. The same if you experienced lack of love from your mother. We are our brothers' and sisters' keepers!

In the process of healing, things always get worse before they get better. First you stir up the residue (unconscious memories), in order for those painful memories to rise to the surface. Then comes a period of pain, grieving, anger, depression, hopelessness, and/or confusion. Then comes relief, resolution, restoration, and/or reconciliation. If you did the exercises in *Recovery of Your Inner Child*, your soul has already begun to trust you by revealing the wounds locked deep inside your heart.

It was not easy for me to find healthy mentors during my healing journey. This is an important principled value of future TTT centers (having loving men and women hold you as you express your deeper thoughts and feelings). I searched throughout the world to find men and women to demonstrate healthy love and touch. It was a humiliating period in my life. I felt like a beggar for love, and it didn't happen in a peaceful manner. In dark hallways and shadows I walked desperately trying to find a morsel of love and healthy touch.

The process of healing is painful and messy for adolescents and adults. Once again, children demonstrate how we heal. When they get hurt, they cry and need comfort. After that, they feel loved and are free to play. It's really that simple. Yet for us as adolescents and adults, it is very risky to let the shields down, and allow another person into those dark areas of our mind and heart. When we find a safe and loving man or woman who will not judge us when we share our deepest and darkest secrets, then trust is developed, and we may begin the process of grieving the losses of our past.

Once you grieve, you will discover your truth, and by knowing your truth on a gut level, you will become free. Then you will access and discover your hidden, negative core beliefs: "I don't trust any man." "I don't trust women." "I am no good." By experiencing new love, you are then free to make new decisions about life and love, changing the script and imprints of your life: "I choose to trust men and women." "I am of value." "Love is always available for me."

The only way out is through. First you need to feel your pain with a trusted man or woman, and in that state of grief ask yourself, or let him or her ask you: "What was the truth about this situation? Who was really at fault? What did I come to believe about myself and others as a result of this experience?" In that moment, where your heart, mind, body, and spirit converge, you will find your deepest core truth and be freed from your personal prison, and find your way home, once again, for the first time. Paulo Coelho's *The Alchemist* details such a journey.

• •

"And the end of all our exploring will be to arrive where we started and know the place for the first time."
—T.S. Eliot, Little Gidding, Four Quartets, *1942*

• •

This process cannot be done alone. I cannot state this important principle enough: *What was born out of broken relationships needs to be healed in healthy relationships.* Bring light into the darkness, together with a torch bearer—the spirit of God and, as psychiatrist Alice Miller stated, a "sympathetic witness." There you will experience the light and freedom from shadows of the past. If you do not have safe people in your life to revisit your wounds, in the future you will be able to stop by one of our TTT centers. We will be there to help you heal and achieve your heart's desire—to be heard, held, and loved (details about this in the conclusion of the book).

When we are "out of touch" with our needs, we become beggars for love, getting bits and pieces in whatever ways or through whatever means possible, i.e. sex (sex with multiple partners, porn, compulsive masturbation), material gain, achievements (we call these "performance-based behaviors" because they give us a temporary sense of fulfillment while still leaving us feeling empty), substance abuse, etc. Others have many walls around their hearts. *In some instances it may look like boundaries, but they are actually walls.*

When we are out of touch with our thoughts, feelings, and needs, or are not being honest with those close to us (family and friends), then we may use sex as a means to get back into our bodies and souls, attempting to reconnect to ourselves once again. Using self-sex or sex with another may act as a reparative drive, an attempt to get back "in touch" with ourselves.

"If it bleeds it leads" is the mantra of the media. Why is the news mostly sensational, reporting accidents, abuse, murders, rapes, wars, and catastrophes? These events represent our shadow side—the unresolved pain within each one of us, that which we have not dealt with. We slow our cars down on the road to view accidents (often called rubbernecking) and say, "Oh" and "Ah," and feel so bad for "them!" It may be difficult for us to cry about our own situation, but at the movies we grieve for the painful lives of others. *Some view another person's misfortune so they don't have to feel or face their own; while others are awakened to their own humanity by seeing the hurt of their fellow man.*

• •

If you do not own it, you cannot move it.
If it is not yours, you cannot move it. You cannot
"make" people do what you want them to do.
You can only change yourself.

• •

Some people of faith, who go through a conversion experience, may then arrive at a second phase called "emotional bypass." This occurs when such a person goes from his wounded or false self and immediately attempts to live through his higher self. Yet, while trying to always be "good" and do the right thing, he denies his wounded parts—the secrets hidden in the recesses of his mind and heart—and lives a seemingly more pious, and perhaps false life.

He may judge himself, others, and/or become self-righteous. Many such persons end up doing what they do not want to do—engaging in self sex, porn, or sex with others outside of marriage.

This creates an ongoing cycle of unmet needs, doing what she or he does not want to do, feeling guilty, and the cycle begins again and again. Resolving your wounds, and fulfilling your unmet love needs in healthy relationships, will not only help you heal, but heal the world as well.

• •

We are both saints and sinners. In order to heal the world, you must actively heal yourself. St. Augustine wisely stated, "Pray as if it all depends on God. Act as if it all depends of you." Focus on the SOLUTION, NOT THE PROBLEM. I may have pressed them, but they are your buttons! When you are triggered by someone else, they are resurrecting your unresolved issues.

• •

Another means of healing relationships is directly within the family. If your parents are alive, capable, and willing, you may consider a Family Healing Session. I have facilitated hundreds of Family Healing Sessions over the past twenty-four years, helping parents, children, and siblings resolve longstanding issues and experience greater love and intimacy. This has been one of the most rewarding practices of my career.

I learned this remarkable therapeutic technique from Dr. Martha Welch, author of *Holding Time* and former professor and researcher at Columbia University (I greatly softened her approach which will be explained later). In just two days, years of strife and regrets are washed away, replaced with bonding and new-found intimacy, as well as skills to last a lifetime. I have trained other therapists in this extraordinary technique. Contact our office if you are interested in a Family Healing Session.

A Journey of Understanding

We have a precious son who struggles with his sexuality. He is very sensitive and an amazing artist. All three of our sons are bright, strong, goal-oriented, and kind.

After years of hiding and keeping secrets, our son told us about his struggles, and we were completely at a loss how to help him. We didn't know how to respond, how to react, what to say or where to turn. We watched him suffer. We saw his frustration. It was so painful for us to watch and feel so helpless.

We believed that God did not create this magnificent man to struggle in this way. However, he didn't know where to turn for answers. After hitting rock bottom, he reached out to a friend who he thought might have battled in a similar way. It was true. His friend told him about Richard and the books he had written. This friend said his own healing journey began with his parents.

That was the beginning of our family healing. Our son led us on a journey of realization and understanding. A journey that helped all of us to experience hope and greater love. We got involved in parenting classes, read many books, and joined a support group. We came to understand how our parenting had impacted our son's wounded heart.

His friend's parents suggested we have a Family Healing Session, that it would help resolve past issues and bring everyone closer. It was a scary proposition, but we knew in our hearts it was our next step of the journey. We asked our two other sons to be a part of the Family Healing Session. "Please do it for us," we requested; and they agreed.

While traveling to the family session, we were all full of "What if's" and "What the heck are we getting ourselves into?" We, as parents, were worried and had no clue what to expect. We had prayed our entire lives, but extra prayers were definitely required before this session. We asked God to lead us ALL. And boy did He!

It is our belief that God led Richard to every thought, word, and action, as well as that of his co-therapist, Phillip. Our family session was full of open hearts, open minds, and honest feelings. There were difficult and painful wounds we had to unearth. We spoke of things never before said, and we processed through them all with love. Everyone was so raw, real, and honest. It was a safe place for us to share our pain, anger, and needs. We were never more proud of all of our sons than in those moments. We believe this family session was a giant steppingstone in our journey of healing and changing unhealthy behavioral cycles in our family. We are so grateful for the guidance, insight, knowledge and healing we experienced in the family session with Richard and Phillip. Thank you is inadequate!

This journey is not a sprint but a marathon, and we continue to see blessings that have manifested as a result of our Family Healing Session. Our sensitive son is receiving counseling and his growth is amazing! All members of our family will push towards increased understanding of ourselves and each other. God will continue to lead and we have renewed hope.

—Joshua & Wendy

*This is a battle of love.
Whoever loves the most and the longest wins!*

Now that you have unearthed hurtful memories, and have begun a program of grieving the losses of your past, please remember this important lesson: *Take time to smell the roses! KISS: Keep It Simple Stupid!* Rest. In our world today, it is almost a badge of honor to be stressed and busy. This is neither admirable nor healthy. It leads to dis-ease of the body and soul. Mix up the healing work with fun. Honor you playful, creative, and spiritual inner child. Get out and do some fun activities with your partner, friends, or on your own. Balance is important, maintain both shadow and light energies in your life.

Stage Five: Healing same-sex wounds

Finding my father's love

One sunny afternoon in Seattle in 1988, my parents visited my wife, our two children, and myself (our youngest son had not been born at that time). For the first time in my life I shared with them that I had experienced childhood sexual abuse from Uncle Pete. My father became enraged and said, "I'm going to kill him. I will find him and make him pay." I said, "No you won't. That is my responsibility. I appreciate your concern dad. Please let me handle this."

After sharing this shocking news, I asked my mother, wife, and two kids to give dad and me some alone time. I remember their hotel room so vividly. There were many windows in the back of the room, and a large arm chair where my father sat. I walked up to him and said, "Dad, even though you are 72 and I am 35, please hold me in your arms. I never remember you holding me as a child. I need this now."

I jumped onto my father's lap and put his arms around me! Remember, this is a former Marine who grew up in military school. Once a Marine always a Marine. He had never experienced the warm embrace of his parents' love, so this was foreign territory for him. Additionally, he was not a fan of tears, as he had decades of repressed hurt and pain lodged deep in his soul.

With my head planted firmly on his chest, I began to grieve uncontrollably. He tried to stop me. "Dad, please, just let me cry. I know it's not easy for you to hear. Please just listen. You don't need you to do a thing. Just hold me. I really need this to heal and grow into manhood." He listened as I proceeded to grieve and heave more deeply. I saw pictures of my past, sexual scenes of people I had hooked up with during my teens and early twenties. "Dad, did you think I wanted sex with them? I was just looking for your love in their arms!"

More tears, many more tears. Then I felt his tears streaming down his face. In that moment he became my Dad, and I became his Son. We bonded for the first time in our lives.

—Richard

Of course, it doesn't happen for everyone in such a manner. Some parents are not safe enough, others may have passed away, while others would never allow their children to get that close. That's OK. You may find a trusted mentor, friend, "Second chance father," or someone at a TTT center to grieve with and receive the gift of healthy touch. I had three male mentors who also held me in their arms as I grieved the losses of my past. My father was unable to sustain this intimacy, it was just too frightening for him, as his own inner child was frozen and locked away deep in the recesses of his psyche.

Please follow the same protocol as mentioned in the previous section—Recall, Revisit, Release, Realize, Resentments, Real love, Renew—only this time resolving father-son, mother-daughter, or any other wounds incurred by someone of the same sex.

SECTION ONE—TIME

Family Healing

a. Create a new paradigm and picture for your family: 13 Rs
b. There are twelve people in one marriage!
c. Spend time with your partner and children (if you have them)

TIME is the way that children experience their value and self-worth, the substantial way that parents invest in and prioritize their children. Love is spelled TIME for every child. Remember the words of Brent Henderson's song: "Love is spelled time. It's something you spend, not something you buy. Before it's too late, I hope you will find. In the eyes of child, love is spelled time."

a. Create a New Paradigm and Picture for Your Family

Thirteen Rs of our Family of Origin*

In a marriage or committed relationship there are two very diverse lineages coming together. *Unless both partners are conscious of their past, they are doomed to repeat it.* Here is a simple yet profound exercise for couples. Each partner writes a history of his or her family of origin based on the 13 Rs listed below. After completing the list, share it with your partner and then make a *new list*, creating conscious choices how you wish to raise your children. Make a new map for the future generations.

1. **Roots**: Multigenerational transmission of unresolved family issues, i.e., alcoholism, drug addiction, sexual abuse, physical abuse/violence, emotional/mental abuse, sexual problems, suicide, depression, mental illness, divorce, prejudice, resentments toward men/women, abortion, illegitimacy, adoption, etc.
2. **Race**: Cultural and ethnic background: African-American, Caucasian, African, Asian, European, Latino, Middle-Eastern, Canadian, Australian, New Zealand, Bi-racial, etc.

3. **Relationships**: with mother, father, siblings, relatives—four types of families:
   - Rigid: distant, disengaged
   - Enmeshment: codependent, engulfed
   - Flexible: open, sharing
   - Combination of all three
4. **Roles**: hero, rebel, loner, scapegoat, clown, princess, golden child, etc. Gender identity—accepted as a boy or girl?
5. **Rung**: Birth Order—oldest, middle, last, only child, odd child out.
6. **Rules**: Overtly and covertly communicated (the shoulds and should nots): sex (good, bad, don't speak about it), money (good, bad, substitute for love, saving, spending, accountability, no accountability, tithing), food (good, bad, not enough, substitute for love), religion (good, bad, toxic, legalistic vs. love), secrets (alcoholism, violence, abuse, abortion, homosexuality, affairs, murder, disease, death, etc.), cleaning (compulsive, sloppy, balanced).
7. **Rhythms**:
   - Fast: stressful, tense atmosphere
   - Relaxed: take time, easy going atmosphere
   - Flexible: relaxed or fast as necessary
8. **Rituals**: Birthdays, holidays, special occasions (Mother's Day, Father's Day, family days, etc.)
9. **Routines**: Meals (together or not); trips (family time, husband and wife time); shopping; family meetings; wake up time; bedtime; entertainment; fun; sports, etc.
10. **Religion**: God of love vs. God of judgment and legalism; guilt and fear vs. love and acceptance; values/ethics/morals vs condemnation and judgment. Different Faiths: Catholic, Christian, Buddhist, Islamic, Jewish, Hindu, Shinto, etc.

11. **Revenue**: Family was rich, poor, had enough, enough was never enough, money always a problem, complaining, content.
12. **R's Education** (reading, writing, arithmetic): Opportunities of learning, lack of opportunities, encouraged, discouraged, realized dreams, unactualized dreams.
13. **Relational** (Personality Styles):
    - Sanguine, choleric, melancholic, phlegmatic (Four temperaments described in Talk section)
    - Emotional/intuitive, spiritual, intellectual, athletic, kinesthetic, artistic
    - Myers Briggs: 16 personality styles (Myers Briggs described in the Talk section)
    - Enneagram: 9 personality types (Enneagram described in the Talk section)
    - Explorer, builder, director, negotiator (Helen Fisher's four temperaments described in the Talk section)
    - Love languages: affirmations, physical touch, acts of service, quality time, gifts (Gary Chapman's Love Languages described in the Talk section)

Exercise

Make a goal when you wish to begin and complete writing out your 13 Rs. Give yourselves a specific date to finish, i.e. two weeks, one month. Then come together, review each other's list, and finally make a new list comprised of family traditions you consciously choose to bestow upon your children and future generations. The combined *New Family Plan* will have lasting benefits for generations to come.

*Seven of the Rs are taken from the article "Family-of-Origin Therapy within Sex Therapy," Claude A. Guldner, ThD, *Family of Origin Therapy: The Family Therapy Collections*, James C. Hansen, Senior Editor, Aspen Publication: Rockville, Maryland, 1987, pages 60-61.

b. Twelve People in One Marriage

There are twelve people in every marriage. "Why twelve?" you ask? "I thought there were only two people." Yes, two people, but each person has six different parts of her or his inner world:

- Higher Self / False Self
- Loving, Nurturing, Encouraging Inner Parent / Critical or Judgmental Inner Parent
- Playful, Golden, Spiritual Inner Child / Wounded and Needy Inner Child

All six parts multiplied by two individuals equals twelve people in each marriage bed and relationship! Unless you become *conscious* of the different parts of your personality, you will continue to blame the other person for your issues. *Therefore, it is critical for each partner to become increasingly conscious of his or her inner family.*

Healing is about resolving issues and becoming *conscious*, knowing if I am speaking from my higher self, false self, loving parent, critical parent, golden child, or wounded child. *When sharing with your spouse, always be in touch with your inner family and know who is speaking to whom!* Otherwise, you may either blame the other person for your problems, or attack them, projecting your own unresolved issues onto her or him.

Equally important is understanding your partner. While upset, is she acting from her wounded inner child, critical parent, or false self? If she is operating from her wounded inner child at the moment, do not share important issues with her or try to speak rationally. Otherwise you are setting yourself up for disappointment.

If the conversation gets too emotional and you don't feel safe, you may ask for a time out and remove yourself from the situation. Suggest coming together again later, when cooler heads prevail. *Know who you are speaking to at any given moment.* It's not easy.

However, practice consciousness, for yourself, your partner, and your family. If you have an immediate issue that you need to share, you may request, "Dear, I have something very important to share with you. Are you able to be in your adult self now?" If she says, "Yes," and you sense that she is able to shift to her higher-self, great, proceed to share. If she is not capable of being in her adult self at the moment, then it is not safe or advisable for you to engage in communication.

Twelve People in One Relationship.

© Richard Cohen, M.A., 2019

You may wish to copy this diagram and place it on your refrigerator, or make copies so that you may reference it when sharing with your partner. Never accuse her or him. Ideally you are both reading this book and doing the exercises together. Then you may support each other through mutual respect and understanding.

Twelve People in One Relationship Blaming Each Other.

© Richard Cohen, M.A., 2019

The more you learn about yourself, and your inner family, the more loving you may be towards your partner. Remember, self-love or self-loathing both work their way outward. Just like we use a thermometer to gauge our temperature, so too, take your inner temperature when sharing with your spouse:

- Am I speaking from my higher self: loving, compassionate, understanding?
- Am I speaking from my false self: blaming and accusing?
- Am I speaking from my nurturing parent: supportive and encouraging?
- Am I speaking from my critical parent: judgmental and condemning?
- Am I speaking from my golden child: loving, fun, embracing, joining?
- Am I speaking from my wounded child: blaming, hurting, withdrawing?

Practice. Practice. Practice. Practice being conscious of who is speaking to whom. Again, there are twelve people in one relationship. Practice consciousness together. The more responsible and conscious you become, the more love you may share with your partner. That love will then overflow to your children.

c. Spend Time with Your Partner and Children (if you have them)

Here are some simple suggestions for couples to practice:

1. Pray together in the morning and in the evening. Couples who pray and play together, stay together.
2. Date weekly. It's important to keep your relationship alive. When you go out on a date: do not discuss kids, money, or politics. Dating is a time to nourish your relationship. Demonstrate healthy touch, enjoy great sex, and please each other. On one date, do what she likes. The next date, do what he likes. Alternate and join with your partner's desire.
3. Listen and share. Practice effective communication skills (list of communication skills in Talk section).
4. Touch, not just in the bedroom, but all the time: healthy non-sexual hugging and kissing; show hugs and kisses in front of your children.
5. Go away together without your children several times a year—weekends are fine. Nourish your relationship.
6. Naked holding and cuddling in the bedroom, and of course make love. Make sure that each partner is in his or her High Self first. No inner children, critical parents, or false selves are allowed when the adults are having sex!
7. Little things count—they add up for better or for worse. Be conscious and attentive to your partner's needs.
8. Water the flower/your spouse: Air (communication), Sun (affirmation), Water (affection). If you don't have it, don't give from an empty tank. Nurture your own inner family before giving to your partner. Build relationships with wise men and women who love and accept you just as you are.

9. Greet your partner when you first walk into the house, before greeting the kids. You are Mr. & Mrs. God to your children. The best gift for children is to see their parents loving each other. Teach by example. "Do as I say, not as I do" is NOT how it works!

10. "Aspirations can be taught, but they're often rejected when listeners see the teacher's behavior is different from their instruction. Values, on the other hand, are transmitted. What we are, in open and in secret, is what the next generation will catch and carry. 'What they see is what they get'" (Clewett, Curtis, *3G: The Art of Living Beyond Your Life*, CreateSpace, 2017, page 58).

Time with your children:

Swiss child psychologist Jean Piaget stated that the developmental task of childhood is play. Research has shown that couples and families that play together, stay together, and are much healthier. Do fun things together.

Suggestions for Parents and Children:

1. **Make goals**: While our children were growing up, on January 1st, we would meet and share our goals for the year, specifying if they were about relationships, school, or professional activities. We would read our goals monthly, to keep them fresh in our minds. In December, we would review our goals, noting how well we did at achieving them. Then on January 1st, we would share about our progress, and tell about our new goals

for the coming year. This was a great family activity that promoted growth and accountability. It gave our children a sense of purpose and direction for their lives, that has continued throughout their adulthood.

2. **Family Fun**: Also on January 1st, each person wrote on a small piece of paper fun activities that she or he would like to do throughout the year. Each person had two or three choices. Each activity had to be reasonable, low budget, and something we could do within a day or two. Then we folded our papers and put them all in a bowl. After this we passed the bowl around and each person chose one piece of paper. We started from oldest to youngest, or youngest to oldest, reading aloud the activity. The first one would be our January activity. The next one would be our February activity, and so on, until we had picked activities for each month of the year. Then we decided upon the weekend to do our fun things. Some examples were the following:

3. **Go Exploring**: On a Saturday or Sunday, we all piled into the car. We started with the youngest child. He would say, "Turn right." Then we continued to go straight until Jessica, our middle child, would say either "Left" or "Right." All five of us would continue until we reached an incredible new destination that we had never explored before. What fun, and it always was! We discovered new lands within hours of our home. It was always a great adventure.

4. **Learn a new song**: This was inspired by the *Sister Act* movies. We would take a popular song and learn it together as a family, with a sort-of-a mock performance in mind. We were spectacular, well, at least in our own minds!

5. **Create Fun Adventures**: We would travel to Ocean City, the Chesapeake Bay, or other nearby bodies of water. Sometimes the trips would last just one day, or we would overnight at a very reasonably priced hotel/motel. We were on a tight budget back in those days. A few fond memories: My wife went to the bathroom before we walked down the steps onto the beach from the boardwalk. Alfred was in his baby stroller at the time. Jarish, Jessica and myself took off our shoes before going onto the sandy beach. All of a sudden the stroller began to roll down the stairs! We watched it as if it were a slow-motion picture, reaching out to grab it, but alas it was already in flight. The stroller must have done two revolutions in the air! Thank God, Alfred was strapped in. The stroller landed on the soft sand, and about twenty mothers tore at lightning speed to comfort our crying infant! Alfred was just fine. We three were stunned and thankful he was OK. Fortunately, Mom was not there to see this scene…

Another funny memory was renting a bicycle surrey on the boardwalk. Jessica was peddling, and surprisingly ran over a rather robust young boy!!! You heard me, she inadvertently ran over him! Shocked, in tears, she put her foot on the brakes. His mother came running, and somehow he was perfectly fine, no worse for wear. He laughed, and his Mom said, "Don't worry about it, he's OK!" And off they went... Those memories, and many more, are indelible in our treasure chest of Cohen family outings.

Enjoy adventures with your kids. Today, all three of our adult children travel the world. They love the thrill of adventure, seeing new vistas, or scaling new mountains (both our sons love hiking). Jessica has been to at least 50 countries. Jarish bikes about 60 miles most weekends, scales the Grand Canyon and other national parks, and climbs glaciers. Alfred is oftentimes Jessica's traveling companion, and camps, hikes, and oh yes, is a body builder.

Another indelible memory on January 1st was to watch a special movie together. It was either something very meaningful, like *The Power of One* (which we watched several years in a row), or something totally fun and fancy-free, like *High School Musical*! I remember all five of us laying down on the bed with snacks and laughing a lot.

6. **Visit museums**: Having the blessing of living in the Washington, D.C. metropolitan area, we have the Smithsonian Museums in our back yard. We raised our children to be curious about all things, and to appreciate the fine arts. They continue to visit museums throughout their worldwide adventures, drinking in the beauty of God's creation and man's amazing works of art.

7. **Applaud their team.** My wife and I attended most of our children's sporting events, i.e. soccer games, baseball games, basketball games, etc. I helped write Jessica's speech as she competed to be the President of her Elementary School, and won! Being there, participating in, and encouraging their passions is good parenting.

8. **Make video calls.** If the father or mother needs to go away for business, military, or mission trips, he or she might want to leave a recording or letters for the partner and children to listen to or read. My wife and children always loved my recordings and notes while I was away. They listened over and over again. It made them feel cared for and loved. Of course, with new technology, we're able to see our families through video conferencing, WhatsApp, FaceTime, and other technological resources.

9. **Share family experiences**: When your children leave home, and perhaps attend university or follow their passions, you may continue communication by initiating a weekly or bi-weekly family call. For the past 15+ years, our family meets every Sunday evening where we all share about our lives. Fifteen years ago, we met via conference calls. Then we switched to Skype. Today we use another video conferencing service. There are many sources of technology to use in order to meet. The main point is to maintain connection and family communication on a regular basis. When we do get together annually for a family vacation, it seems as if we'd never been apart.

These were just a few examples of fun things we did together with our children. Create lasting memories. **Love is spelled TIME.**

Worry tree—put your worries and concerns on a tree after work before you enter your house. Be where you are when you are there. Do not worry about work when you are at home, nor worry about your family when you are at work. Be in the moment. Worry produces no substantial results. Turn worry into love.

Teach your children how to cope with life. Parenting is 95% show and 5% tell. Children learn by example—how you live your life, how you treat your partner, how you manage your daily activities, and how you treat yourself and others, all of these and more are how children learn.

Teach your children basic life skills: how to change a tire, manage money, effective communication skills, conflict resolution (more about these in the Talk section). My wife and I always sat our children on our laps and read books to them. Read them books at nighttime and tuck them into bed while holding them in your arms. For two years every night before bed, I told our children my life story (in 15-minute increments). They couldn't wait for the next night to roll around. It was memorable for all of us.

Teach values through the example of your life. "Do unto others as you would have them do unto you." Demonstrate concern for those in need. Sometimes we drove down to Washington, D.C. and handed out clothing to homeless. Other times my wife took our kids to a food pantry and served food.

A few more suggestions for families:

- If you wish: hold a short morning service: pray together (bless each child before she or he goes off to school), study (inspirational words), help them plan their day, encourage her or him.
- Spend time with each child—make appointments (weekly or monthly)
- Join in her/his world—do what they like to do.
- Show him/her your world—what you like to do.
- Teach skills—give them confidence and competence for life (cars, finances, building, cooking, cleaning, laundry, everyday life skills).
- Bedtime—reading, listening, holding, kissing, praying.
- Family time—meals, rituals (holidays, Sundays, birthdays, holding, etc.).
- Make parent-child times without technology, i.e., no TV, Internet, video games, or movies. The use of technology hyper-stimulates our brains, bombards our senses, and separates us from each other. These days children and youth are hyper-aroused, their physiology is over stressed. They need down time, without cell phones, computers, video games, otherwise they may develop Attention Deficit Disorder and/or easily become detached from others. Do not make TV the center of family life (only on special occasions). Before electricity, families sat around and told stories or read books for hours. Tell stories, play games, and spend quality time together.
- Share meals together. Ask your children about their day. Listen and learn. Current research indicates that families who dine together stay together. Meals and fun are great

diagnostic indicators of successful families. If one child shares a lot, have them be silent and allow the shy or quiet child to share. Create balance and give everyone a turn to speak about her or his day.

- When kids don't want to participate in family activities, strongly encourage them. Eventually they will join in. You want strongly attached children to you, other family members, and friends. Technology is last!

Community Healing

1. Spend time with friends. We need wise men and women who know us and love us just for who we are.
2. Take time for your passions: hiking, fishing, theater, movies, reading, painting, dancing, gardening, cooking, etc.
3. Spend time giving to the community: volunteer work—we gain energy by giving to others.

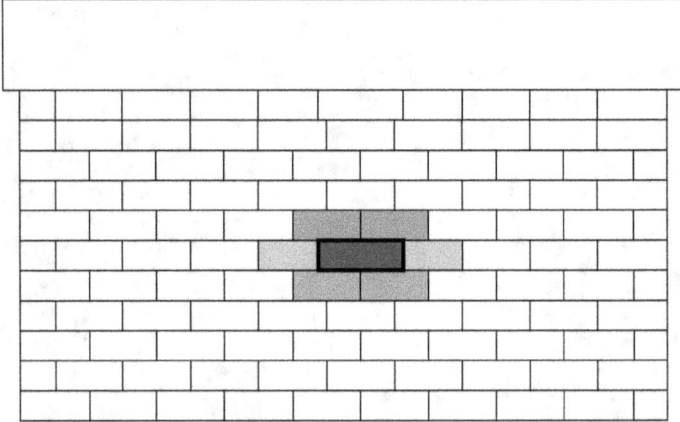

- We need at least two mentors in our lives (the two bricks above us).
- We need at least two friends by our sides, the kind of friends who are *not* overly impressed with us and can speak truth into our lives (the bricks to the left and right).
- We need two people below us, those we mentor, giving to the next generation.

• •

If you don't have at least six or more relationships around you at all times, then you are "off the wall!"

• •

Giving to others generates positive energy and breaks us out of our own depression. There are seniors who need help. The police and fire departments need volunteers. There are multiple ways to help those in need right in your back yard.

4. Maintain a balanced life—heart, mind, body, and spirit. Experience the support/love of God and others. Will power keeps your life moving forward.

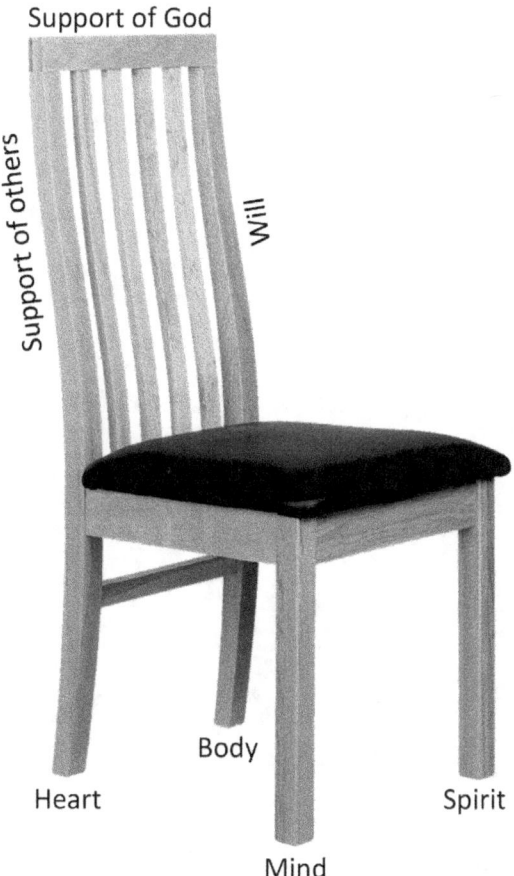

© Richard Cohen, M.A., 2019

Section Two—Touch:

Healing the World through Healthy Touch

He held me in his masculine, strong arms and I melted into his chest. Finally I found the man I had been longing for my entire life. My body melted into his.

She was so sexy and fine. What a great piece of ... I wanted to mount this ... and ... her brains out! This was the woman who knew what I needed, and was willing to please me in every way. It was my time, and she was fine, ready to please my every desire.

Sound familiar? These are the lines in many erotic novels or on porn sites that spin a multi-billion-dollar industry each year. Pornhub, one of the world's largest Internet porn sites, made an estimated $115 billion in 2018 with 100 million visitors monthly. Many people are so horny for sex, so hungry for someone to please them and meet their every sensual need. If only true love, sex, and intimacy were that easy, there wouldn't be: 1) a multi-billion-dollar porn and erotica industry, 2) a 50% divorce rate, and 3) sexual infidelity in marriage by 33 to 75 percent of men and 26 to 70 percent of women (*The State of Affairs*, Esther Perel, Harper Collins, 2017).

TOUCH is like water for all relationships. Without water we die. Touch is the most important of the five senses, and the most neglected. Because there is great confusion between sex, love, and intimacy, we have been denied the natural benefits of healthy touch in our daily lives.

We are born with skin hunger as infants. If those primal needs went unmet in early childhood, if we were misused, abused, or neglected, we may spend the rest of our lives looking for love in unhealthy relationships or behaviors: porn and masturbation for men, romance novels and erotica for women, and hooking up for sex for both men and women.

We must learn how to give and receive healthy touch on a daily basis with family, friends, faith community, and co-workers. *We must venture out from the safety of stroking our pets to embracing our fellow men and women!* (Yes, having pets is a wonderful thing, extending that love to others is the next step.) Let me show you how to touch in safe and healthy ways that will bring hope and healing into your lives and into the lives of your loved ones.

• •

> Those who did not securely attach or connect to their parents or primary caregivers in early infancy and/or childhood, require more touch as adolescents and adults. Most people seek sex to fulfill this primal need for bonding, belonging, and attachment. The problem is that sex never fulfills this basic need, because it is that of a child, not an adolescent or adult. Therefore sex obstructs the very thing that she or he is looking for—to belong, to bond, to attach, to be loved for who she or he is, not for what she or he does. Only healthy touch will do.

• •

Cold Mother, Warms Arms

My mother was cold, judgmental, and aloof. I chased after women from my teens through adulthood. I had lots of sex with many women. I was too afraid to commit. Women would consume or control me, and I didn't trust them at all. Then by chance, or so I thought, I met Samantha. She didn't take my crap. She was different from all the other women that I had known. Sam was a full-bodied woman, and full of love. One time when I was curt and pissed off, she grabbed me, held my cheeks with her gentle hands and said, "Todd, how do you feel? How do you feel?" She looked straight through me.

For some odd reason, I started to cry, and I couldn't stop. Sam held me in her arms. I couldn't stop crying. We sat down on the sofa and she put my head on her bosom. That was the first time in my life that I felt safe with a woman! This was the first of many times when I would break down with Samantha and she would just hold me in her arms. It was as if I was melting away so many layers of self-protection that I had constructed to survive. This woman had so much love for this broken and damaged man. She didn't judge me, she just loved me as I was.

So began my journey from a man who used woman as sex objects, to become a man who appreciates the beauty and femininity of women. No longer am I screwing around. Samantha and I dated for a while longer. It became evident that she was more of a mentor and healthy feminine role model than a girlfriend.

> I continue to heal my mother wound through inner child work, and by relating to healthy women. I am forever grateful to Samantha for sharing the gift of real love.
> —Todd

Home = Love. If you experienced being warmly embraced and supported in the bosom of your family, this will become the normal bonding pattern for all adult relationships. If you experienced any form of abuse or neglect in childhood, i.e. emotional, mental, physical, and/or sexual, these negative bonding patterns become the template for all adult relationships.

Additionally, Location = Love. Hometowns symbolize unconscious, cultural bonding patterns. If you live in a different part of the country or world, you may gravitate to a locale that feels like home, because Home = Love, for better or for worse.

"Many of the here-and-now conflicts people have with their spouses, lovers, ex-lovers, bosses, partners or children are in part emotional reenactments of suppressed feelings stored from incidents that happened when they were children. The same unresolved conflicts they had with their parents always seem to 'mysteriously' reappear in their adult relationships" (Bloomfield, Harold, *Making Peace with Your Parents*, New York: Ballantine Books, 1983, page 9).

Let me personalize these concepts. The first adult I bonded with was my Uncle Pete. As I mentioned, both my father and mother were unsafe. Before Uncle Pete introduced sex into our relationship, he played with me, shared with me, listened to me, and I felt loved. Then everything turned south through sex.

Later in adolescence and early adulthood, unconsciously I was looking for men who mirrored my Uncle's characteristics: warm, fun, physical, and compassionate. Why did all these men, who were either homosexually or heterosexually oriented, keep leaving me? I didn't understand that I was resurrecting the same personality in different men! My inner child kept trying to get them to stay, but alas each one of them left (just like Uncle Pete).

This is called a negative bonding pattern, whereby our unconscious sets the agenda for failed adult relationships, one after another. You may ask, "Were you demanding too much from them, is that why they left?" Perhaps that was true in a few instances, but mostly these were men who simply needed to be needed. Several had a messianic complex, wanting to save others while unwilling to face their own issues. Therefore, they were not capable of sustaining a long-term mutual friendship.

I lived in an upper-middle class Jewish community outside of Philadelphia. Externally we seemed to have it all, but there was constant fighting and battles. Many of my friends' parents were also fighting, separated, or divorced. The safest person in my life, after Uncle Pete, was our housekeeper Ophelia. She felt more like a mother to me than my own mom. She took me to her home on many weekends. It was wonderful to escape from my tumultuous family. The highlight of each visit was attending her church. It was so warm, welcoming, and loving. I was the only little white boy in a sea of African-American families!

Today, my wife and I live in a community where almost 70% of the population are African-Americans, and 99% of our church members are black. It feels wonderful. Unconsciously we are always trying to go "home," recreating both positive or negative bonding patterns.

All relationships are an attempt to give and receive love. You may be unconsciously attracted to certain people, attempting to restore or reconnect with those from your past. This is one reason why people often marry someone who mirrors the abusive parent or caregiver. It is their inner child trying to change their parent, through their partner, to finally get the love which was never experienced at home. Dr. Harville Hendrix calls this the "Unconscious Marriage." We are all crazy for love! Let's learn how to break these negative bonding patterns and experience healthy love.

Many of us do not really know what we need. We long for intimacy and yet may fear it at the same time. Sex is familiar. Sex may feel safe. Sex can be quick and lack intimacy—get off and get out because of guilt, shame, and/or fear of intimacy. Married men are having sex with other women or men. Married women are fantasizing about other men or women, and/or having sex with them. Singles are hooking up and getting off as well. But are they truly fulfilling their deeper needs for love?

Men think it is normal to view women's bodies in a sexual manner, looking at their breasts, butts, and other body parts. There is nothing normal about this. Actually, when we sexualize another person, we are objectifying him or her, turning them into sex objects. *Of course, appreciating beauty is wonderful, but sexualizing is demeaning.*

Both men and women are handsome and beautiful. Beauty is to be appreciated. However, the next time you sexualize a man or a woman, think about this: What if I am looking at my son, daughter, nephew, niece, or another loved one? Do I really want to sexually objectify my family member and relatives? Do I want to sexually objectify my son or daughter, aunt or mother, brother or father? In essence, that is what we are doing.

Both men and women have sexual issues: compulsive masturbation, pornography, lusting after women's or men's body parts, and/or sexual relations outside of marriage. *All of these behaviors are driven by unhealed wounds and unmet love needs.* Men may have experienced insufficient bonding with their mothers while growing up, and women may have experienced insufficient bonding with their fathers. I call this an Opposite-Sex Attachment Disorder (OSAD). It lays the groundwork for potentially failed relationships, and/or objectifying members of the opposite sex. If we successfully bonded with our father, mother, grandparents, and other relatives, and thus internalized their love, then we would have no need to objectify another human being. That would constitute disrespect for our loved ones.

I will now provide simple solutions for separating Love, Sex, and Intimacy—which became all meshed up way back when—through the power of healthy touch.

TOUCH

Self-Healing
- Stats about Internet Porn
- Science of Healthy Touch
- Exercises for Healthy Touch

Family Healing
- Stats about Marital Infidelity
- Stats about Teen Sexual Activity
- Touch Program for Couples
- Touch Program for Children
- Touch Program for Relatives

Community Healing
- Touch Program for the Community

Self-Healing

This is an emergency!

Time magazine published an amazing article entitled *PORN and the Threat to Virility: The first generation of men who grew up with unlimited online porn sound the alarm,* on April 11, 2016, authored by Belinda Luscombe.

Continuous use of Internet porn accompanied by masturbation leads to Porn-Induced Erectile Dysfunction (PIED) in men.

> "A growing number of young men are convinced that their sexual responses have been sabotaged because their brains were virtually marinated in porn when they were adolescents" (p. 42).
>
> "And compelling new research on visual stimuli is offering some support to the young men's theories, suggesting that the combination of computer access, sexual pleasure and the brain's mechanisms for learning could make online porn acutely habit forming, with potential psychological effects" (p. 42).
>
> "Teen girls increasingly report that guys are expecting them to behave like porn starlets, encumbered by neither body hair nor sexual needs of their own" (p. 42).

Gary Wilson, former adjunct professor of biology at Southern Oregon University, is the author of *Your Brain on Porn* and creator of the website www.yourbrainonporn.com. He has given several TED talks about the damaging effects of porn. Watch his TED talk, *The Great Porn Experiment* at: https://www.yourbrainonporn.com/about/your-brain-on-porn-in-the-news/garys-tedx-talk-the-great-porn-experiment-2012/.

2018: Pornhub (world's largest Internet porn site) annual views 33.5 billion; 100 million views daily; approximately $115 billion revenue! Retrieved from: https://www.pornhub.com/insights/2018-year-in-review

"Philip Zimbardo, emeritus professor of psychology at Stanford University (and the guy who did the famous Stanford prison experiment), notes that porn often goes hand in hand with video games and is similarly finely tuned to be as habit-forming as possible. 'Porn embeds you in what I call present hedonistic time zone,' he says. 'You seek pleasure and novelty and live for the moment.'" "'...he says, porn has the same effect on behavior as a drug addiction does: some people stop doing much else in favor of pursuing it. 'And then the problem is, as you do this more and more, the reward centers of your brain lose the capacity for arousal'" (p. 46).

How Porn is Changing a Generation of Girls, *Time*, April 11, 2016, p. 47

Adapted from *Girls & Sex*, Peggy Orenstein, 2016

"Watching natural-looking people engaging in sex that is consensual, pleasurable and realistic may not be harmful—heck, it might be a good idea—but that is generally not what the $97 billion global porn industry is shilling. Its producers have one goal: to get men off hard and fast for profit. That means eroticizing the degradation of women. In a study of behaviors in popular porn, nearly 90% of 304 random scenes contained physical aggression toward women, who nearly always responded neutrally or with pleasure. More insidiously women would sometimes beg their partners to stop, then acquiesce and begin to enjoy the activity, regardless of how painful or debasing."

After extensive studies, experts are now saying that Internet Pornography is the crack cocaine of pornography and is a growing epidemic that will forever change our society. Please do not read the following statistics as simply numbers. They represent millions of real people, many are children. Retrieved from *Child-Proofing on the World Wide Web: A Survey of Adult Webservers, 2001, Jurimetrics. National Research Council Report, 2002.*

Internet Pornography Industry

- Internet pornography industry generates $12 billion dollars in annual revenue. This is larger than the annual combined revenues of ABC, NBC, and CBS. *~Family Safe Media, January 10, 2006*
- According to the Florida Family Association, PornCrawler, their specialized software program, identified 20 U.S. companies that accounted for more than 70 percent of 297 million internet pornography links.
- By the end of 2004, there were 420 million pages of internet pornography, and it is believed that the majority of these websites are owned by less than 50 companies. *~LaRue, Jan. "Obscenity and the First Amendment." Summit on Pornography. Rayburn House Office Building. Room 2322. May 19, 2005*
- Business practices of commercial internet pornography sites:
  - 74% display free teaser porn images on the homepage, often porn banner ads.
  - 66% did not include a warning of adult content.
  - Only 3% required adult verification.

Children Internet Pornography Statistics

- The average age of first exposure to Internet porn is 11. *~Family Safe Media, December 15, 2005*
- 90% of 8-16 year old's having viewed porn online mostly while doing homework.

- The largest group of viewers of Internet Pornography is children between ages 12 and 17 ~*Family Safe Media*
- Child pornography itself generates $3 billion annually. ~*TopTenREVIEWs*
- There are an estimated 100,000 websites offering illegal child pornography

Internet Pornography Surfing Habits

- Of all university students polled, 87% have virtual sex mainly using Instant Messenger, webcam, and telephone. ~*CampusKiss and Tell" University and College Sex Survey. Released on February 14, 2006. CampusKiss.com. February 17, 2006*
- More than 32 million individuals visited a porn site in Sept. of 2003. Nearly 22.8 million of them were male (71 percent), while 9.4 million adult site visitors were female (29 percent). ~*Nielsen/Net Ratings, Sept. 2003*

Christian Internet Pornography Figures

- 51% of Pastors say Internet pornography is a possible temptation; 37% say it is a current struggle; *4 in* 10 pastors have visited a porn website. ~*Christianity Today, Leadership survey, Dec 2001*
- Of those polled at a Promise Keepers event, 50% said they had checked out pornographic material within the past week.
- One in six women (17%) including Christians, struggles with pornography addiction. ~*Today's Christian Woman, 2003*
- Almost half of Christians surveyed said pornography is a major problem in the home.

Jason Chen, June 1, 2010

1. 12% of the websites on the Internet are pornographic = 24,644,172
2. Every second, $3,075.64 is being spent on porn.
3. 40 million Americans are regular visitors to porn sites. Seventy percent of men ages 18-24 visit porn sites in a typical month.
4. In the U.S., Internet porn pulls in $2.84 billion per year. The entire worldwide industry is worth $4.9 billion.
5. 2.5 billion emails per day are pornographic. That's 8% of all emails.
6. Twenty-five percent (25%) of all search engine requests are pornographic related. That's 68 million per day.
7. Top porn search terms: sex 75 million / adult dating 30 million / porn 23 million.
8. Utah has the nation's highest online porn subscription rate per thousand home broadband users: 5.47.
9. Thirty-four percent (34%) of Internet users have experienced unwanted exposure to porn either through pop up ads, misdirected links or emails.
10. There are 116,000 searches for "child pornography" every day.
11. The least popular day of the year for viewing porn is Thanksgiving. The most popular day of the week for viewing porn is Sunday!

Retrieved from: https://gizmodo.com/5552899/finally-some-actual-stats-on-internet-porn

Mind-Blowing Porn Stats

1. Porn sites receive more regular traffic than Netflix, Amazon, & Twitter combined *each month*. (HuffPost)
2. 34% of internet users have been exposed to unwanted porn via ads, pop-ups, etc. (WebRoot)
3. People who admit to having extramarital affairs were over 300% more likely to admit consuming porn than those who have never had an affair, according to a 2004 study in *Social Science Quarterly*.
4. The most common female role stated in porn titles is that of women in their 20's portraying teenagers. (Jon Millward.) (*In 2013, Millward conducted the largest personal research study on the Porn Industry in the U.S. He interviewed 10,000 porn performers about various aspects of the business.*)
5. Recorded child sexual exploitation (known as "child porn") is one of the fastest-growing online businesses. (IWF)
6. 624,000+ child porn traders have been discovered online in the U.S. (Innocent Justice)
7. Between 2005 and 2009, child porn was hosted on servers located in all 50 states. (Association of Sites Advocating Child Protection)
8. Porn is a global, estimated $97 billion industry, with about $12 billion of that coming from the U.S. (NBC News)
9. In 2016 alone, more than 4,599,000,000 hours of porn were consumed on the world's largest porn site. (PH Analytics)
10. Eleven pornography sites are among the world's top 300 most popular Internet sites. (SimilarWeb)

Consumer stats from NCOSE *that are hard to believe:*

11. 64% of young people, ages 13–24, actively seek out pornography weekly or more often. [1]

12. Teenage girls and young women are significantly more likely to actively seek out porn than women 25 years old and above. [2]
13. A study of 14- to 19-year-olds found that females who consumed pornographic videos were at a significantly greater likelihood of being victims of sexual harassment or sexual assault. [3]
14. A Swedish study of 18-year-old males found that frequent users of pornography were significantly more likely to have sold and bought sex than other boys of the same age. [4]
15. A 2015 meta-analysis of 22 studies from seven countries found that internationally the consumption of pornography was significantly associated with increases in verbal and physical aggression, among males and females alike. [5]
16. A recent UK survey found that 44% of males aged 11–16 who consumed pornography reported that online pornography gave them ideas about the type of sex they wanted to try. [6]

Retrieved from: https://fightthenewdrug.org/10-porn-stats-that-will-blow-your-mind/

Romance Novels and Erotica for Women

The Economist, May 26th 2016, by K.S.C.

In 2013, the Romance Writers of America (RWA) estimated that sales of romantic novels amounted to $1.08 billion, and accounted for 13% of adult fiction consumed that year, outselling science-fiction, mystery and literary novels. In the five years to 2015 in Britain alone, romance and erotic fiction sold 39.8 million physical books worth £178.09 million. In fact, the RWA estimates that 84% of romance-book buyers are female, and 41% are between 30 and 54 years old. A recent Nielsen study reported that around 15% of the genre's fans buy new books at least once a week; 6% do so more than once per week.

SECTION TWO—TOUCH

Retrieved from: https://www.economist.com/blogs/prospero/2016/05/erotic-and-romantic-fiction

Who are romance novel/erotica readers?
- 84% are women and 16% are men
- 70% of the readers are 18-54 years of age
- 80% of the readers are Caucasian, 6% Hispanic, 7% African American, 3% Asian, and 4% others
- How they found books: 24% in store display, 12% on TV, 10% Author's website, 18% online browsing

Retrieved from: https://www.nielsen.com/us/en/insights/news/2016/romance-readers-by-the-numbers.html

• •

I hope that many of these statistics shocked you, as they did me. So many men and women are hooked on Internet porn/erotica, and don't know what to do. I do, and that is what TTT is all about: solving the porn, romance novels, and erotica epidemic with healthy solutions for you and your loved ones.

• •

"Be in touch."
"Keep in touch."
"You're out of touch, I'm out of touch."
"The final touch!"
"Untouchables."
"Reach out and touch someone."
"Touchy feely."
"He's / She's so touchy."
"Reach out and touch, somebody's hand, make this world a better place, if you can." (Nickolas Ashford, Valerie Simpson, 1970.)

Scriptural references to healing and healthy touch:

- Matthew 14:3-6 Those who touched him were healed
- Matthew 19:14-15 Jesus placed his hands on the children
- Psalm 68:4-6 Father to the fatherless, puts the lonely in families
- I John 4:7, 12, 16, 18, 19-21 Love each other as God loves you. No fear in love
- John 13:23-25 A disciple leaning on Jesus
- Luke 12:48 Those given much, much is required
- Luke 6:30 Give to all what they ask
- Matthew 25:40 What you did for the least of these, you also did for me
- Matthew 16:19 Keys to the kingdom: loose on earth, loosed in heaven, bound on earth, bound in heaven
- Matthew 5:4 Those who mourn will be comforted

Time, Touch & Talk Restored Me

As I reflect upon our sessions of *Time, Touch & Talk*, I am filled with a deep spirit of gratitude. A counselor introduced me to your work at a time when I was experiencing a great deal of grief—a feeling of being stuck and not knowing how to get beyond it. Over the years many fine counselors, for whom I am most grateful, had helped me with issues of severe depression and low self-esteem by taking time to pray and talk through various life experiences. When we first met, I felt like Lazarus who had been delivered from a deep pit of death. However, the old burial clothes of shame, guilt, fear, terror, anger and rage still needed to be removed by someone who was willing to get close enough to actually touch these feelings and help me beyond these debilitating emotions. This part of the journey definitely called for more than talk.

Your ministry of *Time, Touch & Talk* has begun to melt these feelings coming from early childhood traumas. Because of many traumatic life experiences, I was filled with incredible amounts of ambivalence—yearning to be held in a wholesome, affectionate way by a loving father but so afraid of being ridiculed, rejected and eventually abandoned for being so needy. You made it very clear early on that God is the true healer and that you are ministering God's unconditional love through *Time, Touch & Talk* in order to be present to the whole person—body, mind and spirit. At last it felt safe to begin to investigate those very painful feelings and memories and bring them into God's healing light. It is amazing how the gift of physical holding and touch almost immediately began to melt away the many layers of repressed feelings that have kept me from being the man God has created me to be. So many of the feelings come from a pre-verbal period in my life and therefore demand more than talk. The results of working through these repressed emotions has left me with greater self-acceptance, a deeper sensitivity for relatives and friends and thus a deeper connection to God.

For me the experience of *Time, Touch & Talk* has been an incredible on-going gift. Since you have experienced similar life traumas, you know and understand the pain. From your knowledge and experience you have always

> ministered to me with genuine caring, by freely expressing words of affirmation as well as meaningful physical touch. This gift has always been given in an atmosphere of safety, honesty and non-judgmental respect—which together add up to God's unconditional love.
>
> Thank you so much for being so brave as to face your own demons as well as having the courage and willingness to answer God's call to help others remove debilitating burial clothes. May God bless you Richard, as well as your family and ministry.
>
> —Gerald

THE SCIENCE OF TOUCH

The skin is the external nervous system and the largest organ in the body. "Touch is the most important, and yet the most neglected, of our senses" (Colton, Helen, *Touch Therapy*, New York, NY: Kensington Publishing Corporation, 1989, page 14). We can live without sight, sound, taste, and smell. But we cannot *survive* without touch as infants and children, and we cannot *thrive* without touch as adolescents and adults.

The skin represents 12% of our body weight. There are 5 million touch receptors in the skin. *We are all born with skin hunger.* We learn information through skin touch with our parents and other caregivers. This helps our brain develop.

The physiology of touch and how we learn as infants and children:

1. We receive stimuli through the touch sensors
2. This sparks a minor electrical charge that creates a neuron response

3. There are hundreds of billions of neurons or nerve cells in the body; each separate from the other, and connected by synapses
4. The electrical charges from one neuron to the other communicate like Morse code
5. They send messages through the spinal cord to the brain

"Touch stimulates the production of chemicals in the brain, and these feed our blood, muscle, tissue, nerve cells, glands, hormones, organs. Deprived of touch to stimulate these chemicals, we may be as starved as if we were deprived of food" (Colton, Helen, *Touch Therapy*, page 16). Endorphins, a chemical released in the brain after being touched, reduces stress and generates a sense of wellbeing. Touch stimulates all the body's systems: respiratory, circulatory, digestive, muscular, eliminative, nervous, endocrine, immune, and reproductive systems.

"Dr. Rene Spitz, working at a hospital for abandoned babies and babies whose mothers were in prison, became alarmed that even though the infants were well-fed and kept in highly sanitary conditions, they suffered a high rate of disease called *marasmus*, a Greek word meaning 'shriveling up or wasting-away of the flesh without apparent medical cause'" (Colton, Helen, *Touch Therapy*, page 43). Yet, babies being raised in third world countries with less sanitary conditions were thriving. Why? Because women from the community would come in daily and rock the babies, while talking and singing to them. "Touched babies thrived, while those who were left alone in bassinets tended to become ill, their cells dying of touch starvation" (Spitz, Rene, *The First Five Years of Life*, New York: International Universities Press, 1965).

Some researchers believe that babies who were touch deprived, witnessed violence, or were violated may be predisposed to violence as adolescents and adults.

> "We can receive no greater assurance of our worth and our lovability than to be affectionately touched and held in the cradle of family life" (Colton, Helen, *Touch Therapy*, page 58). "One learns to love not by instruction but by being loved" (Montagu, Ashley, *Touching: The Human Significance of the Skin*, New York: Harper and Row Publishers, 1986, page 38).

The Puritanical heritage of the USA taught us to equate touching with sex. As Queen guitarist Brian May said in the movie Bohemian Rhapsody, "Americans are puritans in public and perverts in private!" This Puritanical heritage and hypocrisy has created generations of detached, oversexed teens and adults. The porn and romance novel industry, erotica, and entertainment industries bank on our being "out of touch" with our core needs for connection, and foster an oversexed culture of teens and adults.

Many fathers become frightened when their daughters develop into shapely women during adolescence. Instead of dealing effectively with their sexual feelings (which may lead to guilt and shame) and moving through this phase with the help of their wives or friends, they withdraw from their daughters. These daughters then seek male affection and affirmation by using their bodies, dressing provocatively, to sexually attract men. Fathers please keep embracing your daughters! Keep hugging them, otherwise you are abandoning them into the arms of young men who will use them sexually because you failed to affirm your daughter's femininity.

Today, people are imprisoned in their skin because of touch deprivation or inappropriate touch in infancy and early childhood. The skin acts as a barrier that shuts them in and keeps others out.

Touching becomes an assault on their being and integrity. We have created a nation and world of Pelvic-Phoebes—fear of touching the pelvic area of another person—who are *Touchphobic*.

My experience with sexually addicted clients, is that they fear intimacy because closeness equals pain. Others who are resistant to physical intimacy are protecting themselves through the armor of their skin and become Touchphobic.

Two men propagated systematic detachment between parents and children in the late 1880's through the 1930's. Their names were Dr. Luther Emmett Holt and Dr. John Broadus Watson of Johns Hopkins University. They wrote books on parenting stating:

1. Don't use a cradle (in other words, don't rock your baby)
2. Don't breast feed
3. Don't spoil your child by touching him or her
4. Let the child sleep alone

Their advice was literally followed throughout the world. Here are quotes from Dr. Watson's book, *Psychological Care of Infant and Child*, New York: Norton, 1928: "There is a sensible way of treating children ... Never hug and kiss them, never let them sit in your lap. If you must, kiss them once on the forehead when they say good night. Shake hands with them in the morning. Give them a pat on the head if they have made an extraordinarily good job of a difficult task. Try it out. In a week's time you will find how easy it is to be perfectly objective with your child and at the same time kindly. You will be utterly ashamed of the mawkish, sentimental way you have been handling it" (Montague, Ashley, *Touching: The Human Significance of the Skin*, pages 150-151).

It boggles the mind! Of course, two men wrote such nonsense. Women would have much more love and compassion towards children.

The brain develops two-thirds of its growth by the end of the first year of life, and 90% of its growth by the end of the third year of life. Premature and C-section babies have more problems with attachment. An infant needs at least thirty minutes of bonding with his or her mother after birth. The baby needs a minimum of twelve months breast feeding for secure attachment. Cribs are not ideal because the child is accustomed to the rocking sensation in the womb. Babies need to be carried, caressed, cuddled, cooed, and rocked.

Untouched infants may either rage and become angry for life, or emotionally shut down for life—they may have either no motivation, drive, desire, connection—or become angry or fearful of people and life.

Dr. Montagu writes in his book *Touching*, that lack of touch *or* unhealthy touch creates:

- A biochemical imbalance in the body
- Increases the amount of masturbation in adolescents and adult
- Violence in children and future adults
- Potentially leads to addictive behaviors

Dr. Sydney Jourard studied touching among European and American friends in public places (restaurants, etc.). Europeans touched over 100 times in an hour. Americans touched about 2-3 times in an hour. The Puritanical Heritage has maintained that Touch = Sex, a great lie that has been propagated until the present time. We are massively touch deprived. Many have sex just to be touched.

And yet, there are massive inhibitions for non-sexual touch among family and friends. Many believe that:

- Parent-child touch = potential sexual abuse or may create a homosexual child (especially father-son relationship, which is not true at all)
- Sibling touch = potential for incest
- Same-sex friends = potential homosexual behavior
- Opposite-sex friends = potential adultery or sexual behavior
- Casual friends = potential for promiscuity

"The opioid epidemic is a uniquely American problem. While the U.S. accounts for about 5 percent of the global population, its residents consume about 80 percent of the global supply of prescription opioids … It's not that Americans experience severe injuries or suffer from chronic pain at notably higher rates than, say, Europeans, according to experts" (Retrieved from: https://news.yahoo.com/americans-much-pain-141918964.html / January 30, 2019).

"There were about 300 million pain prescriptions written in 2015," Irina Koffler, senior analyst, specialty pharma, Mizuho Securities USA, told CNBC. "The 300 million pain prescriptions equal a $24 billion market, Koffler said, but it's not a market evenly divided around the globe" (Retrieved from: https://www.cnbc.com/2016/04/27/americans-consume-almost-all-of-the-global-opioid-supply.html).

• •

We are numbing ourselves through medication, porn, erotica, romance novels, compulsive masturbation, and affairs largely due to touch deprivation.
It is epidemic and pandemic.

• •

We may fear touch and intimacy with others for many reasons, some of which may be:

1. If I extend my arms to hug you, will you think that I am coming onto you?
2. If I hug you or you hug me, perhaps I may become sexually aroused, which would be extremely embarrassing.
3. If I hug someone of the same sex, he and/or others may think that I am, or we are gay.
4. I may experience fear of being close to you: intimacy and touch creates vulnerability which may be painful because of my past unreconciled wounds.

The closer you get to others, the more you may hurt because the walls around your heart will melt and the wounds of the past may emerge (a totally unconscious occurrence). This may be why we push those closest to us further away.

I will never forget one man who came to me for help. He was married with five children, and was a sex addict. On the way home from work, he would stop at a public park and have sex with multiple partners. This would happen many times per week. When he was leaving my office, I asked if he would like a hug. He stepped back, and emphatically said, "No!" No, I wondered? And then I remembered the principle stated above: intimacy for some equals pain. Anonymous sexual encounters are much safer for them.

We fear that which we do not understand. The best way to conquer fear is to understand and then take action.

Touch: How? When? Where? With whom? What does it look like?

Religions traditionally encourage marital fidelity, frowning upon breaking that commitment to one's partner by engaging in sex outside of marriage. This is not an arbitrary rule God imposed for punishment, but is meant for our health and wellbeing while maintaining a sacred covenant. We are intended to first learn intimacy with others before engaging in sex. Healthy touch is safe, non-sexual, and produces a sense of calmness, connection, and wellbeing.

Let's start with the basics:

We need various forms of Healthy Touch during different developmental stages:

Bonding (0-1½ years): Mother-Child, cuddling, full body contact, eye contact, smiles, breast feeding. From this we gain a sense of trust and wellbeing. This sets the template for all future relationships. We need the same bonding activities with our fathers, minus the breast feeding of course!

Separation-Individuation (1½ -3 years): Now the parents establish boundaries. The first stage of life is bonding, and the second stage of life is boundaries to protect the child from harm. *Bonding and Boundaries, Love and Limits.* The parents allow the child to separate and individuate, establishing her or his own identity. Now the child learns to crawl, walk, and talk. The child's operative word is "No" as he or she realizes, "I am not you."

> In stage one, the infant is symbiotically one with mother. Now his brain cognizes that he is separate and different from his mother. The child develops a sense of will and initiative. During this phase, the parents hold the child, and let go, hold and let go. They continue to hold, establish eye contact, smiling, kissing, cuddling their toddler affirming her autonomy while maintaining healthy boundaries—so she doesn't burn her hand on the stove or destroy the house!
>
> As the son recognizes the physiological differences from his mother, he needs to inherit his sense of masculinity and gender identity from his father. The daughter, although she

too will separate and individuate, continues to gender identify with her mother.

Socialization, Questions/Answers (3-5/6 years): The main operative question of the child at this stage is, "Why?" He or she develops an understanding of cause and effect thinking. Hold, let go, hold, let go. The radius of relational influence is expanded to siblings, relatives, close family members, and friends. The child needs hugs, kisses, and playfulness.

Boys need to move through the Oedipal stage—letting go of his mother to be with his father. A healthy father and mother relationship helps the boy navigate through this process of letting go of his mother. The son continues to gender identify with his father through roughhousing, wrestling, hugging, pats on the back, arm around the shoulder, and showering together.

The daughter needs to move through the Electra stage—letting go of her father to be with her mother. A healthy mother and father relationship helps the daughter navigate through this process of letting go of her father. The daughter needs to continue gender identifying with her mother, internalizing her femininity, through a continued and close relationship. She admires her mother, wishing to emulate her.

Latency (5/6-12/13 years): Rules and Reasons. Touch: Homosocial bonding through play with same-sex relatives and friends:

Boys: play sports, rough and tumble, horse play, video games, etc.

Girls: relational, friendships, sports, etc.

The pre-adolescent child gains a sense of gender identity through homo-social activities—boys with boys, and girls with girls. They belong to their tribe of same-sex peers.

Same-sex siblings should help, but may prevent healthy gender identification.

Fathers and sons: horseplay, wrestling, shared activities. Father teaches his son skills.

Mothers and daughters: teach skills, share time together.

Father: affirms his daughter. Mother: affirms her son.

Adolescence (12/13-18/21) Identity, Autonomy: Hetero-social (opposite-sex) bonding and mentoring: now there is a great need for him or her to have opposite-sex mentors, i.e., aunts, uncles, grandparents, teachers, coaches, etc.

Homo-social mentoring: same-sex role models, i.e. relatives, teachers, athletic coaches, etc.

Touch: hetero-social bonding in public with mentors (boys with female mentors, and girls with male mentors). There will be a strong need for opposite-sex mentoring and healthy touch during this phase as the teen navigates through puberty and bodily change—arm around shoulder, holding hands, hugging.

The adolescent will reprocess through any of the previous stages of development which were not achieved. He may continuously work to individuate from father, mother, or other family members.

She or he will need healthy, safe, non-sexual touch. Otherwise she or he may seek sex as a substitute. Their bodies are going through significant hormonal changes and she or he experiences a natural skin hunger for healthy touch. Either she or he will experience touch in healthy ways or through sex. *We as their parents, family members, and community decide their outcome.*

As infants, toddlers, and small children, we need to be held in order to feel safe and secure in the bosom of our family.

By experiencing healthy touch with our parents, relatives, and caregivers, we internalize a sense of secure attachment. If this does not occur from infancy throughout early child development, or we experience insufficient bonding with our parents and loved ones, we may spend the rest of our lives seeking to obtain that connection through sexual relations with members of the same or opposite sex.

• •

The parent-child relationship rules the world, rules every personal and professional relationship. What was once experienced as a normal need for bonding with our parents in pre-adolescence, will become sexually charged after puberty. Sex then becomes the driving force to fulfill unmet love needs. Once again, those normal needs for bonding with mom and/or dad will never be fulfilled through sexual relations, porn, erotica, or masturbation because they are the legitimate needs of the child within. Only healthy touch will heal our mind, heart, and satiate our bodily hunger for secure attachment.

• •

Underneath everything we do, is a need to *belong*. Marilyn Monroe is a classic example of this principle. She was looking for her father's love through the admiration of men. It never worked because all she wanted was to be loved for who she was, not for what she did, or how she looked. Despite becoming a sex symbol and cultural icon, her troubled personal life and tragic suicide is a cautionary tale.

Touch deprived women may read romance novels, hook up with many partners, and/or use erotica and masturbate.

Sexualizing men (or women) represents a false attempt to fulfill childhood needs for love and bonding. Women want and need to be cherished by a man. They need to internalize daddy's love, grandfather's love, uncle's love, and brother's love. If not, they shall continue to seek acceptance by offering their bodies to men.

Touch deprived men hunger after breasts, butts, and vaginas. They seek their mother's love and acceptance by sexualizing women. Other men may hunger after men's bodies and penises. They are simply seeking their father's and/or same-sex peer's love and acceptance. If only sex healed those needs for real love! However, it always interferes with the fulfillment of one's true desire, because it is the desire of a child, not an adult.

Please follow the formula for proper self-care as detailed in the first section on Time. This will allow you to reclaim your inner child, who holds the key to the kingdom of heaven within.

TOUCH ≠ SEX

Once again: Affairs, sexual activity outside of a committed relationship, compulsive masturbation, all are used as *false attempts* to heal wounds and fulfill basic love needs, and *sex will never fulfill those deeper needs.*

> "From early childhood, boys learn to suppress their emotions, while girls learn to express and manage the complete range of feelings. Small wonder that by the time they grow up, meet, and marry, men and women are so often at opposite ends of the spectrum when it comes to the importance they place on expressing feelings. A man is more likely to equate being emotional with weakness and vulnerability because he has been raised to *do* rather than to voice what he feels" (Gottman, John, *Why Marriages Succeed or Fail . . . And How You Can Make Yours Last*, New York: Simon and Schuster, 1994, page 143).

"First, the male's autonomic nervous system, which controls much of the body's stress response, may be more sensitive and take far longer to recover from emotional upset than does the average female's ... Second, men may be more reactive because even when they withdraw from an argument, they are more likely to repeat negative thoughts that keep them riled up. If you could read their minds, you might hear phrases like, 'I don't have to take this crap,' or 'It's all her fault,' or 'I'll get her back for this.' Such inner scripts, whether of righteous indignation or innocent victimization, are clearly not self-soothing. Compared with a woman, it seems to be much harder for a man to relax his guard and say, 'Honey, let's talk about'" (Gottman, page 147).

"A particular difficulty for men is sharing their feelings, being emotionally intimate. Women are generally more able to express their feelings. Men are more activity-centered, not emotionally centered. Many men learn very early in life that it is socially unacceptable to express their feelings. Another reason is the physiology of the male. Men are prone to cut off because of their physiology. Emotional arousal is more punishing on the male system due to their hormones; consequently, they learn to cut off and shut down from an early age" (Welch, Martha, *Holding Time: Intensive One-Day Seminar*, audio cassettes, 1996).

"The right and left hemispheres of the male and female brains are not set up exactly the same way. For instance, females tend to have verbal centers on both sides of the brain, while males tend to have verbal centers on only the left hemisphere. This is a significant difference. Girls tend to use more words when discussing or describing incidence, story, person, object, feeling, or place. Males not only have fewer verbal centers in general but also, often, have less connectivity between their word centers and their memories or feelings" (Jantz, Gregory L., Brain Differences Between Genders, *Psychology Today*, February 27, 2014, https://www.psychologytoday.com/us/blog/hope-relationships/201402/brain-differences-between-genders).

Most men, as boys, were taught *not* to feel, or else they were teased, mocked and called names on the playground of life. Then as teenagers and adults, they become *dickheads*. You heard me right, most men are *dickheads*! They have sex on the brain much of the time, because they are shut down between their genitals and their brains, where we experience our emotions and feelings (in the region of our stomach, solar plexus, and heart). Therefore, many men are *dickheads*, which is neither normal, nor natural. This is because of emotional disconnection. I am not saying that all men are *dickheads*, just the vast majority, as witnessed by the staggering porn and infidelity statistics.

The Birth of the Dickhead

Some boys shut down emotionally as children and may become a Dickhead, out of touch with their feelings and potentially sexualizing their repressed emotions.

© Richard Cohen, M.A., 2019

Married men are expected to be sensitive to the needs of their wives and children. This may be a contradiction to their upbringing, thereby promoting frustration for both men and women. Many men were trained to become *dickheads*. They are out of touch with their feelings; they had to bury them alive because:

They were called names when expressing their feelings on the playground while growing up. "Boys don't cry." They had to suck it up. "You're a sissy for crying." It wasn't safe for boys to express their normal and natural emotions.

The physiology of boys is more punishing than girls when they are hyper-aroused. Boys are built physiologically to be emotionally sensitive. They are easily aroused, just like their genitals. They get upset quickly, and if allowed to move through and express their feelings, they will become calm, healthy, and happy campers. If they are called names and told, "You're a sissy," "Boys don't cry," then they emotionally shut down and the only feeling they will be entitled to express is anger. Then the connection between the genitals and head kicks in, and Voila! Another *dickhead* is born!

> "As our boys grow older, we may not only skimp on the amount of physical affection we give them but unwittingly limit the amount of affection they give others. Following a masculine code that is thousands of years old, we raise our male children to be tough, resilient, and independent. We tell little boys as young as three or four years of age, 'Tough it out,' 'Play with the pain,' 'Stop that bellyaching,' 'Stop being a sissy,' 'Figure it out for yourself,' 'Don't come crying to me!' 'Defend yourself!' and 'You're acting like a girl.'
>
> "If we go against the mainstream and encourage a boy to be gentle and caring, he is likely to be the target of verbal abuse on the playground. Sensitive and affectionate boys—boys who have the very qualities that most women say they would like in

their husbands—are often labeled 'wimps' or 'sissies' or worse behind a thick skin. It's no wonder that when they grow up to be men, they require less affection than women and are less likely to dole it out. Like plants that have to withstand the rigors of a cold climate, they've been hardened off" (Love, Patricia and Robinson, Jo, *Hot Monogamy*, CreateSpace, 2012, page 186).

We need to re-educate men to feel, and touch is a simple vehicle to achieve this goal. *Men are visual. Women are verbal.* Remember, in general they were punished for displaying any kind of genuine emotions. They need to be taught how to feel once again. This does not mean that we want to turn men into women. We need to awaken their natural sense of emotions in order to heal and become real men. *Real men feel!*

Women were allowed to express their feelings, except in many dysfunctional families. It was generally acceptable for girls to cry, laugh, and touch. They were however, often prohibited from displaying anger. That was a "boy" emotion, and it wasn't acceptable for nice girls. Women need to reclaim their power by displaying anger in healthy ways. Chronic anger is always a mask hiding a hurting heart. Acute, momentary anger is for the purpose of self-protection. It is healthy to protect ourselves and our loved ones. Anger is a primary emotion, along with fear and love. And the greatest of these is love. "Perfect love casts out fear" (I John 4:18).

• •

Women, please help your man get back in touch with his emotions through healthy, safe, non-sexual touch. Men will initially become sexually aroused, and that's OK. What goes up must come down—it's just blood in a shaft! He doesn't need to ejaculate each time he gets aroused. Focus on healthy, safe, non-sexual touch.

• •

Exercise for married couples

Two to three times per week, cuddle naked with your partner for ten minutes. Do not have sex at those appointed times. Have sex on different nights or times of the week. Men may easily get sexually aroused. That's fine. Leave it alone and it will go home! Re-educate the body to experience healthy touch sans sex.

Men who did not successfully bond with their fathers, brothers, and other boys in early childhood and pre-adolescence will need to experience healthy, non-sexual touch from other men. Women who did not successfully bond and connect with their mothers will need to experience healthy, non-sexual touch from other women.

If a same-sex attracted man comes onto a heterosexual man, or a same-sex attracted woman comes onto a heterosexual woman, it is a compliment. He or she is attracted to the masculinity or femininity that he or she sees within you. It is not about sex, it is about a need for bonding and internalizing that which was not sufficiently experienced in early stages of child development.

The Art of Hugging

> ### The Hug that Changed My Life
>
> When I look back and try to recall the best journey of my life, I think of one that was special for me. Traveling is my passion. I have visited many countries around the world. The cities I have seen impressed me and painted my mind with different colors. Now, with time and distance, I can say that these colors have the same intensity. They are still woven in the tapestry of my life.
>
> However, there was one journey that has left the greatest impression. It was a profound journey which led me into the core of my own personality. The path was quite scary and dark. The only tool I took with me was faith and trust in the process. Many times I wanted to give up. I was hurt and overwhelmed. However, as it happens in life, the greatest value is born out of adversity. Observing my own inner world allowed me to see my fear of intimacy, touch, and authenticity. Parts of myself that I didn't know existed appeared. The greatest example for that was meeting my inner child. It was very touching and special.
>
> When I think of myself five years ago, unsupported by my own family, lonely, and distrustful, I see a boy terrified of intimacy and touch. For me, a hug was a pathetic gesture with unknown meaning. I often wanted to escape when I was supposed to hug another person. Hugging was just a mechanical action for me. I was detached from my own body and from other people. During my therapy with Richard I learned how to hug someone in a meaningful way.

One particular hug was a life-changing experience that I will never forget. That hug was a physical and metaphysical encounter. Until then, I would not allow myself to be vulnerable with another person. However, for the first time in my life, during that hug I felt like an adult-son being embraced with a father's acceptance and understanding.

I would like to explain the mechanics of the hug because of its impact and intensity. Richard put his arms around me, and I did the same. The position of the arms was important. He put his right arm over my left shoulder and his left arm beneath my right arm. With open hands he supported my back. His head slightly touched mine and I did the same. We connected. I allowed myself to experience being embraced, which lasted a few minutes. I closed my eyes so I could feel it better. The connection was on all levels: physical, emotional, mental, and spiritual. It was authentic. I had a feeling of giving a piece of myself to another person, and being vulnerable. After that experience nothing was the same.

The hug I experienced that day with Richard inspired me to intensify my journey and learning process. I practiced how to express my feelings and needs in all relationships. I learned how to say "No" and set healthy boundaries with unsafe people. I am still learning to be more authentic and less "a good boy" or "pleaser" who fulfills other's needs before his own.

For years being "a good boy" was my survival mechanism. Now I have learned to trust myself more, listen to and accept the needs of my inner child. The path I

> traveled and continue to travel is thorny and lengthy but extremely rewarding. I appreciate all the gifts I have received on my path of healing. Nowadays, I am a more fulfilled man, much more awake and aware. My life is enriched with meaningful relationships full of love and support, and hugging is now an integral part of my relational vocabulary!
>
> —Robert

The majority of humans are *Touchphobic*. There may be a fear of intimacy with those we know, or those we don't know. Various cultures in the world greet one another in different ways: some shake hands, others give a kiss (or kisses) on the cheek(s) and a short hug, while another culture bows before one another. TTT plans to expand a new tradition of hugging and holding throughout the world.

• •

"We need four hugs a day for survival.
We need eight hugs a day for maintenance.
We need twelve hugs a day for growth."
Virginia Satir, Family Therapist

• •

What does a healthy hug look like? One arm above the shoulder of the other person, and the other arm below their shoulder (not two arms above or two arms below). It's also ideal to hug cheek to cheek. Imagine that your skull has a zipper and is open. Allow the love of God to flow down from heaven through you to bless the other person. Simultaneously, receive God's love from the other, so there is an ongoing flow of giving and receiving love. Let the energy flow between the two of you. Practice this healthy hug for one minute with your partner, parent, or friend. Give and receive.

SECTION TWO—TOUCH

Richard Cohen hugging his son Alfred.

If you are taller than the other person, you do not have to lean over to hug him or her (creating an A-frame hug). Simply bend your knees so that you are both standing cheek to cheek. Bending at the knees allows your lower back to release and is better for your health and posture. Also, do not put your head on the shoulder of the other person. Cheek to cheek, hug, breathe, give and receive, give and receive.

We all crave closeness. Because many are starved for affection, sexual feelings may arise when you get close to either a person of the same and/or opposite sex. This is a natural phenomenon given that most of us are touch deprived, or we experienced a lot of sexual relationships. If while hugging a sexual feeling occurs, simply bring that energy from your genital area to your heart, so men, instead of getting a hard on, get a heart on!

© Richard Cohen, M.A., 2019

Men, when you hug a woman, don't put your head on her shoulder. Keep your head erect and let her head rest on your shoulder, chest, or remain cheek to cheek. Men who, while hugging, put their heads on a woman's shoulder are like little boys trying to get mommy's love. Keep your head erect. No, not that erection, your other head erect! Let her feel secure in your arms. A woman longs for a man to take care of her.

- Touch = worthy = secure = loved.
- More touch = less stress = less fear = greater love.
- Physical touch regulates moods, whether one is hyper-aroused or depressed. It is a natural anti-depressant.
- Healthy touch is a stabilizing factor for infants, children, adolescents, and adults.

SECTION TWO—TOUCH

HUGGING = HAPPY, SECURE CHILDREN, TEENS, AND ADULTS.

Hugging Exercise

1. Begin a program of healthy hugs or holding with your family members and friends. You may want to show them photos of healthy hugs, and practice together.

2. Tell your family members or friends about healthy hugs and set boundaries and guidelines.

3. Practice one-minute hugs, imagining that the top of your head is open, allowing the love of God to pour through you to the other person. Give and receive love. At times, you may play beautiful music in the background. This will allow you to more easily open your hearts toward each other.

4. Again, if you are taller than the other person, bend your knees and release your lower back. Optimum hugs are cheek to cheek.

5. Expect emotions to flow as you keep practicing healthy hugs with safe people, i.e., anger, fear, sadness, pain, etc. Let your feelings out. Let them go. *The more you feel, the quicker you heal.*

6. Expand your radius of safe people to give and receive healthy hugs. The more, the better! Once again, as the brilliant family therapist Virginia Satir suggested, give and receive 12 healthy hugs per day.

As mentioned earlier in the book, when we finally get what we need—healthy touch—we may experience anger and eventually grief. Just be prepared if unexpected emotions arise while practicing hugs with those closest to you.

Holding helps heal the hurting heart.
After the tears comes the sun!

© Richard Cohen, M.A., 2019

Healthy touch allows us to reprocess unreconciled emotions. This will reduce the need for medication and potentially save billions of dollars in treatments that may or may not work. Dr. Martha Welch taught about the science of parent-child bonding and attachment. Through correct parent-child bonding, children who experienced characteristics of autism were healed and became high functioning. Dr. Welch's protocol for parents of children who experienced reactive attachment disorder showed scientifically significant changes in the brain as their bodies and hearts were soothed and able to internalize their parents love. These children became calm and productive in all aspects of their lives (https://nurturescienceprogram.org/martha-welch and https://www.columbiapsychiatry.org/profile/martha-g-welch-md). Just to clarify: Dr. Welch's method is *not* associated with "attachment therapy" which was misused by several incompetent therapists. Dr. Welch always promoted parent-child bonding, never having a child held by the therapist.

Three types of unhealthy hugs:

Three Types of Unhealthy Hugs

A-Frame Hug   Duck Hug   Side-Saddle Hug

© Richard Cohen, M.A., 2019

- A-frame hugs: pelvic area sticking out so they don't touch!
- Duck hugs: patting the back.
- Side-saddle hugs: hip to hip, avoiding the pelvic areas from touching.

All three unhealthy hugs avoid real intimacy and the experience of genuine affection. Practice healthy hugs with as many people as possible. *Healthy hugs heal!*

A family that plays, prays, and displays affection openly, will create happy and secure children. Dr. Martha Welch taught me that if the father and/or mother are away much of the day, it is most important to reattach to their young child or children upon their return. Hold them in your arms. Allow them to express all their thoughts and feelings, and simply say, "Thank you, tell me more." Do not correct or explain. They just need to express their feelings, be heard, and then reattach/reconnect to and with you. It is really as simple as that. However, it may take time until you establish this new routine and rhythm of re-connecting at the end of the day.

In August 1997, the LIFE magazine cover story was entitled "The Healing Power of Touch," by George Howe Colt. In the article he discussed the groundbreaking research of Dr. Tiffany Field at the University of Miami's Touch Research Institute (TRI). Dr. Field has collaborated with researchers from Duke, Harvard and other esteemed universities around the world. "Massage, it seems, helps asthmatics breathe easier, boosts immune function in HIV-positive patients, improves autistic children's ability to concentrate, lowers anxiety in depressed adolescents and reduces apprehension in burn victims about to undergo debridement, the painful procedure in which contaminated skin is removed" (page 60).

"A simple touch—a hand on a shoulder, an arm around a waist—can reduce the heart rate and lower blood pressure … Touch also stimulates the brain to produce endorphins, the body's natural pain suppressors, which is why a mother's hug of a child who has skinned his knee can literally 'make it better'" (p. 60).

"America is suffering from an epidemic of skin hunger," stated Dr. Field. "TRI set up a study in which volunteers over age 60 were given three weeks of massage and then were trained to massage toddlers at the preschool. Giving massages proved even more beneficial than getting them. The elders exhibited less depression, lower stress hormones and less loneliness. They had fewer doctor visits, drank less coffee and made more social phone calls" (page 60). You may wish to read more about the research conducted by Tiffany Field, Ph.D. and her staff at the Touch Research Institute, University of Miami School of Medicine (http://www6.miami.edu/touch-research/Index.html).

"Research has demonstrated over and over again, that patients who are ill, heal much quicker when touched. Nurse Pamela McCoy reported that eighty-five percent of patients that were touched recovered faster and felt better about the hospital staff" (McCoy, Pamela, "Further Proof that Touch Speaks Louder than Words," *RN Magazine*, vol. 40, no. 11, November 1977, pages 43-46).

• •

People need loving the most when they deserve it the least—especially those who demonstrate oppositional behaviors—because they are angry and hurt little children living in adolescent or adult bodies. Touch helps build trust between the giver and receiver.

• •

On a different note, sports represent our need for play, festivity, and pageantry. People scream, yell, shriek, and carry on! It's OK to touch on the field (pat each other on the back, butts, or hug), but it's not OK to touch in real life. Therefore, in some aspects, sports are associated with men's need to be close to one another. Here are the poignant and revealing words of Dave Kopay, former running back for the Washington Redskins, who came out as gay after retiring from the NFL.

"On the field we can get away with all kinds of physical affection men wouldn't risk showing anywhere else. We aren't ashamed to reach out and hug. After a touchdown you see men embracing on the field like heterosexual lovers in the movies. We were able to hold hands in the huddle and to pat each other on the ass. I think these are healthy expressions of affection. What is unhealthy, I think, is that we are so afraid of expressing ourselves in the same way outside of the stadium, out of uniform" (Kopay, David, with Young, Perry Deane, *The David Kopay Story: An Extraordinary Self-Revelation*, New York: Arbor House, 1977, p. 57).

Sports have built-in opportunities for touch that need to be translated into our normal, everyday activities: TTT.

Sidney B. Simon, former professor at the University of Massachusetts, stated, "It's amazing how much work we get done in school when we care for skin-hunger needs first." He suggests various exercises like massage trains and back massages for his students. (Simon, Sidney B., "Please Touch: How to Combat Skin Hunger in Our Schools," *Scholastic Teacher Magazine*, Junior/Senior High Teachers' Edition, October 1974, pages 222-25). Of course, in this day-and-age, touching in the classroom has become taboo. How sad. Instead of promoting the solution, we are legislating the problem.

• •

Once again, there are hundreds of books on parenting and family life, however, few mention the need for healthy touch. This is shocking and sad.

• •

With our *High Tech* society, we need *Increased Touching!* We need more touch than ever before. Loving our pets is wonderful and research shows those with pets live longer. Now let us bridge the gap between affection for our cats and dogs to our fellow man! I will offer suggestions for healthy touch in the workplace. We need to get up from our workstations and computers, and practice the art of healthy hugs.

Sex Sells

You are so sexy. I want your sex. Let's get it on! When we repeat any behavior, it becomes emotionally and mentally wired in our brain as researched in the field of neuroplasticity. Here is the principle:

SECTION TWO—TOUCH

• •

Nerve cells that fire together, wire together.
Nerve cells that fire apart, wires depart.

• •

This works for both healthy and unhealthy behaviors. If we sexualize our basic need for healthy touch, enough will never be enough. Chemicals released in the brain, such as dopamine, will eventually plateau and require a new and heightened level of sexual arousal. Thus the addictive cycle continues.

We can actually use this same principle for healing. Repeated behaviors such as healthy, non-sexual touch, emotionally charge our neural pathways in the brain, releasing a pleasurable dopamine sensation that creates as sense of wellbeing.

Many pop songs have been written about sex. "Sexual Healing," sung by Marvin Gaye, is a classic example of confusing the need for sex, love, and intimacy. Others song simply eroticize emotional needs of love and intimacy, i.e., "I Want Your Sex," George Michael, "Side to Side," Nicki Minaj, "Sexy Back," Justin Timberlake, "You're Makin' Me High," Toni Braxton, "Sexual Seduction," Snoop Dogg, "Sex With Me," Rihanna, "I Touch Myself," The Divinyls, "Justify My Love," Madonna, "Erotic City," Prince.

Many men and women seek and crave love and settle for sex. We seek to love and be loved, we seek acceptance and a place to belong. We engage in sex to connect, but again, sex alone never satiates the deeper needs of the soul—bonding, belonging, connecting. As teens we are taught to have sex, as if this will truly fulfill our deepest desires. *However, teenagers and adults need acceptance and healthy, non-sexual touch first, last, and in between.* Sex is only meant to be shared within a committed relationship. Otherwise, and in every case, it is used as a substitute for love (and oftentimes, within a marriage, it may be used similarly).

How can we separate sex, love, and intimacy? If there are sexual overtones between you and another person who is not your committed partner, check within yourself to see if this feeling is coming from you or the other person. Once again, if it is your energy, bring that sexual feeling up from your genital area into your heart. Men remember, instead of getting a "hard on," get a "heart on!" If you feel the sexual energy is coming from another person and you don't feel safe with him or her, remove yourself from the situation. You may say, "I don't feel comfortable, see you." Or, "Sorry, I have to go now!"

Teenagers and those in their twenties and thirties are in their sexual prime. If they experienced secure bonding in their family of origin and community, their sexual energy will be more easily contained and saved for that special person. If secure bonding and attachment did not occur in the formative years of life, if there was much strife and chaos in their families of origin, they will be more susceptible to sexualize legitimate needs for love and affection.

Learn to implement healthy, non-sexual touch in your daily life. Twelve hugs a day will keep the doctor away.

Many men do *not* know how to touch except for sex. They must be reeducated. Children, adolescents, and adults need healthy, non-sexual touch on a daily basis. Once again, the use of Internet porn, compulsive masturbation, erotica, and sexual hook-ups will never satiate our essential need for real love and connection.

Exercise

Women, please help men get back "in touch" with themselves:

1. Gently hold his checks and look into his eyes.
2. Place your hands on his shoulders and look into his eyes.
3. Put your hands on his chest and look into his eyes.

By touching him, looking into his eyes, and sharing responsibly (use "I" statements, not "You" statements), he will bond with and yield to you. He is waiting to be taught. He needs you to show him the way home. He is lost and is a hungry puppy for love. He just needs a map, instructions, and direction. Women hold the key to a man's heart and love life, as most men don't know what women truly want and need. Train your man and he'll be forever grateful and attentive to *your* needs. It takes time. Be patient. Be good to yourself in the process. Get lots of love and affirmation from your faith, family, and friends. It took years for him to numb out and become a sex animal. Therefore, it will take time for him to get back into his body and reconnect with his heart.

Today so many leaders are falling from grace: Harvey Weinstein, R. Kelly, Kevin Spacey, Bill Cosby, multiple politicians (who can forget Clinton receiving oral sex in the Oval office?), many priests, pastors, and on and on. It is shocking, sad, and shameful what they have done, misusing men, women, and minors. Yet who is providing help and hope for them and the countless other men and women doing the same? Who is providing help and hope for the women, men, and minors who were abused, and now involved in the MeToo# and TimesUp# movements?

Those who commit these sexual crimes are so "out of touch" with their wounded inner children. While in graduate school studying psychology, one of my professors (who worked 25 years in Child Protective Services) taught us that every perpetrator was once a victim of child sexual abuse. They are out of touch with their wounded inner child. Of course, this does not justify the horrific acts of abuse they commit. It just helps us see them as humans not simply monsters. They, along with the victims of abuse, need help to discover, recover, and heal their broken hearts.

• •

Those who need loving the most often deserve it the least.

• •

We continue to recreate our past in present day relationships in order to heal wounds and fulfill unmet love needs. Sounds crazy, but as Harville Hendrix stated, "All adult relationships are an attempt to reconcile our wounded child within."

Taking My Heart Back

She held me in her arms as I grieved the pain of my uncle's abuse. Hilde was like a sister to me for two decades. We helped to reparent one another. One afternoon, I revisited the horror of being a five-year old when Uncle Pete sexualized our relationship. Before that, he groomed me. I never bonded with my father and Uncle Pete became a substitute Dad. We played together, laughed together, did rough and tumble activities together. He won my heart. Then he crawled into bed with me and taught me to have sex with him for almost one year. "This is our special secret. Don't tell anyone about it." Can you imagine a NFL hall-of-fame football player and a five-year old boy?

But the worst was yet to come. I learned to compartmentalize my fun and loving Uncle from the monster who had sex with me each evening. When he said "Good-bye" and moved out, he took my heart with him. You see, as crazy as it may seem, in my child's mind and heart, I truly believed that he loved me. Now the first adult that I bonded with was leaving my life! It was unthinkable.

During this healing and holding session with Hilde, I realized that I gave this man my heart. He took it with him when he left our house, and I had been trying desperately to recreate men in my life who shared similar characteristics like Uncle Pete. I can easily name at least eight men in my life, former partners and then friends, who seemed to be loving, gentle, and demonstrative. Then, just like Uncle Pete, one by one they would leave me.

While being held by Hilde, I had an "Aha!" moment! I had given my heart away to Uncle Pete and was trying to retrieve it with each failed relationship. I was holding each man hostage with my excessive need for their love. They were not leaving me, I was actually pushing them away with my intensity and conscious and unconscious demands.

In that moment, with Hilde's help, I took my heart back from Uncle Pete. "You don't deserve this. It is my heart, and you stole it from me. You used me for your own pleasure and purpose, and then you left me. Now I take my heart back and release you from my life!" I cried for a very long time in Hilde's arms, having retrieved my heart and escaped from emotional prison.

Before this "Aha!" moment, I had done years of therapy to work through the pain of childhood sexual abuse. But this was on a deeper level, at the core of my being. Remember the Layers of Our Personality chart. This experience of giving my heart away to Uncle Pete resided in the core of my being. This was the final piece to receive my ticket out of hell. From then on, I did not expect another man to care for me in such a way. I became my own best friend, protector, and nurturing inner parent. Of course, I will always have a healthy need for male friends and mentors, sans codependency. Today I have several close friends and participate in men's groups. I am surrounded by healthy guys, and we take care of each other.

—Richard

Caution: If you or a loved one experienced childhood sexual abuse, receiving healthy touch may cause both physical and emotional pain. Touch may be experienced as an assault upon one's being. Receiving healthy touch may be scary. Gently introduce a healthy hug to a sex abuse survivor.

Always ask permission before giving a hug to anyone. In the case of sex abuse survivors, expect rejection. Be persistent, patient, and loving. It will take time for the walls around his or her heart to come down. Don't quit. Keep reaching out, keep breaking down the walls of fear and detachment. If you persist, eventually the resistance will wane as trust is built. Again, this will take time.

As a survivor of childhood sexual abuse, I both longed for and feared healthy touch. When receiving hugs from family and friends, I would often become sexually aroused and pull back (thus creating the A-frame hug). I was so afraid the other person might feel or sense that I had an erection. This went on for years. Finally, during my therapy, I told my close friends that I may become aroused while hugging, and asked for their understanding. When we hugged, and I experienced sexual arousal, I told my friend and immediately I burst into tears. It was both humiliating and liberating at the same time. I had to repeat this over and over again for months until I felt safe enough to simply give and receive a healthy hug without fearing or experiencing sexual arousal. In time, I became the king of healthy hugs! So can you, your friends, and loved ones.

Another interesting characteristic of sex abuse survivors is *psychic splitting.* In order to cope with the horror of being sexually abused as a child, the individual learned to detach from her or his body as a coping mechanism. Some were able to watch the event as if they were floating above the scene. As an adult, when confronted with a particular emotional situation either in a personal relationship or while watching a movie, and especially viewing a painful scene, she may detach from her body once again, and join with the protagonist in the scene. This happened to me many times while watching emotionally driven stories at the movies or on TV. I had to learn to take my heart back after the film was over. I went into a bathroom stall, silently spoke to myself and would say, "I am not _____ (name of the character in the movie). I am me. Look. I'm an adult." Then in my imagination, I would reach out to the protagonist and take back my heart—pulling it into my chest. Then I could breathe once again, grounded in my own body. This is a simple suggestion for other sex abuse survivors who easily detach from their bodies.

> One final caution to former abuse survivors: When you are feeling vulnerable, *do not watch* any TV show or movie depicting deeply emotional scenes. Otherwise you may risk becoming entangled and/or enmeshed with the protagonist's pain. The danger is that their pain may go directly into your soul. This entanglement may last for hours or days if you don't figure out whose pain you are experiencing. Therefore, when feeling weak and vulnerable, never read or watch dramas where you will witness the powerful pain of others.

I know this may sound extremely bizarre and strange if you have not experienced childhood sexual or physical abuse, or a profound trauma in your life. For those of us who did, we know what it is like to leave our bodies, or have our body and soul usurped by the pain and experience of others. It takes practice and effort to cut off from the other, get back into our body, and reclaim our own dignity and personhood … which was robbed from us as children. You may read psychologists Hal and Sidra Stone's extraordinary book *Embracing Our Selves* about their remarkable therapeutic technique called Voice Dialogue. Throughout their book they describe those who become possessed because of mental and emotional detachment from their true self. These are secular psychologists understanding this phenomenon from a strictly therapeutic perspective.

Exercise for Healing

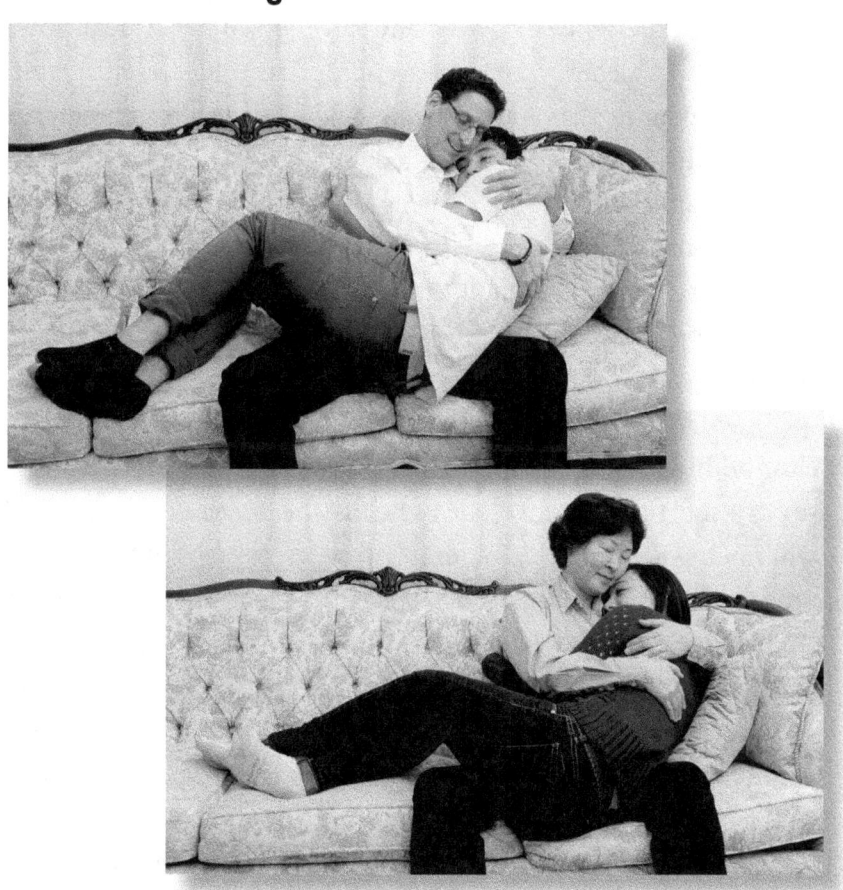

Holding between the mentor and the adult-child.

Here is a beautiful exercise for healing. If you, a loved one, or a close friend was physically or sexually abused, or experienced neglect—a lack of physical touch in childhood—please begin a regular program of holding (see the photos). While sitting on a sofa, the giver is in the parental position (vertical), holding the person who is in the child position (horizontal). The adult-child places both arms underneath the arms of the mentor, completely around his or her back. This clearly establishes a parent-child relationship. If one of the adult-child's arms is above and around the shoulder of the mentor, it creates more of a mutual relationship.

While the mentor holds the adult-child, he may say, "Allow yourself to experience the warm and safe touch of your ideal father or mother (whichever gender is appropriate). Please close your eyes and imagine that you are being held by your ideal parent in a way you always wanted and needed. Or you may imagine a spiritual mentor is holding you, pouring God's love into your body and soul. Just relax and receive." To create a more conducive healing atmosphere, you may play beautiful and soothing music in the background while you hold the adult-child, just as you would hold your own son or daughter.

Practice this on a regular basis. Establish specific times and set clear boundaries. If the adult-child was abused and learned to use sex as a substitute for love, she or he may become sexually aroused while being held. This is a natural and necessary part of the healing process. *Healing happens in the reverse order in which the original wounding occurred.* This means if you were sexualized as a child, had many sexual relations, or practiced years of self-sex, then sexual feelings will emerge while being held by a mentor. *Sexual feelings naturally emerge before core wounds are accessed.* Again, healing takes place in the reverse order in which the wounding occurred—first sexual feelings will surface, and underneath you will discover core pain, hurt, and needs for love.

What I am about to share may sound counter-intuitive: If you truly wish to heal, share with your mentor about being sexually aroused, and perhaps having desires for him or her. Over the past thirty years I have witnessed many in ministry who continue to "white knuckle" it through their recovery, never truly resolving their core wounds or fulfilling unmet love needs in healthy, non-sexual relationships. It is an endless cycle of frustration. Many continue to act-out sexually, feel guilty, only to continue this cycle again and again. This is because their deeper needs for love are never truly met in healthy, non-sexual relationships.

To sincerely heal, one must face his shadows—sexual desires, core wounds, and needs for love. When getting closer to a mentor, ideally the adult-child needs to speak about his sexual desires with and perhaps for his mentor. "I am feeling sexually aroused. This is difficult to say, but would you like me to pleasure you?"

As humiliating as it may be for the adult-child to share these and other sexual thoughts and feelings, the mentor needs to accept this without reacting, without showing signs of being shocked, although he or she may feel this way. The only true response of the mentor will be to offer the gift of unconditional love: "Thank you for sharing. I don't need or want sex from or with you. I love you just for who you are."

This will allow the adult-child to pass through the sexual feelings and access the core wounds lodged deep in his heart. This process of holding, bonding, and releasing pain will take practice, patience, and time. This saved my life, and the lives of countless clients that I have assisted over the past three decades. I have heard amazing stories of transformation from hundreds of men and women. They found marvelous mentors who helped them pass through their guilt, shame, hurt, and pain. Finally, they felt loved, and achieved an incredible sense of freedom.

Caution:

If the mentor experiences sexual feelings while holding the adult-child (we call this countertransference in therapy), never share those feelings with him or her. Bring the feelings up from your genital area to your heart and stay focused on loving the adult-child. After the holding time is over, find a safe person to share about your experience. Process through your feelings. This is an opportunity for you to face your own shadow (unconscious parts of your soul), your needs, and deal with your issues. Refer to many Self-Healing exercises in the section on Time.

If the adult-child experiences sexual feeling while being held, this is a great opportunity for deeper healing. My personal and professional experience over the past 30 years is that beneath your sexual feelings you will find your hurt and hungry (for love) inner child.

"Above all else, it seems to me that it is our role as human beings always to join learning to loving-kindness. Learning to learn, learning to love, and to be kind are so closely interconnected and so profoundly interwoven, especially with the sense of touch, it would greatly help toward our rehumanization if we would pay closer attention to the need we have for tactual experience" (Montagu, Ashley, *Touching: The Human Significance of the Skin*, New York: Harper and Row Perennial, 1986, page xiv).

The Healing Power of Healthy Touch

I began my friendship with Richard many years ago, as he was embarking on his healing journey. Soon after we met, Richard attended a retreat that I was facilitating. This normally professional, well-organized, and responsible man began acting out during the retreat. He was angry, defiant, and rebellious. I knew Richard was engaged to be married, but I did not recognize his inner turmoil or cry for help as he wrestled with his past and faced his future. I only knew that he was making trouble for the program, and for me!

After one gathering that Richard had disrupted, my patience had worn thin. I walked up to him at the back of the room after the program was over, and asked, "Are you rebelling on purpose?" To which he replied, "Yes!" Fortunately, I had received wise counsel from a dear friend, so instead of becoming upset or trying to correct Richard, I simply looked into his eyes and put my arms around him. He literally burst into tears, melted in my arms, and sobbed on my shoulder. We went to a quiet room where he explained how he was in therapy dealing with his sexuality, a source of great conflict for many years. He shared that as his upcoming marriage loomed, his fear of intimacy with a woman, unhealed wounds from his past, and longing for a male mentor's love were welling up within him.

I asked Richard to become my roommate at the retreat. He was so happy to make the move. Every night I held him in my arms, as we shared and became close friends. One night, Richard's response to our intimacy was to come on to me sexually, offering to pleasure me. I was neither attracted nor repulsed by this, and simply told him that I had no such need or interest, that was not what our closeness was about.

When I spoke those words, Richard burst into tears once again. "I just needed to know that I was safe with you, that you wouldn't take advantage of me like my Uncle did so many years ago." It helped him begin to distinguish between the sexual pleasing that he had learned and believed he needed to do in order to be loved, and the genuine intimacy and male bonding that he was deprived of in childhood. As our friendship grew, Richard and I remained roommates, sharing an apartment for several months after the retreat.

As Richard learned and grew in his therapy, he shared his insights and began to mentor me in my own pursuit of healing and wholeness. Some months later I met a very shy woman who was moved by a presentation that I gave about the confusion between sexuality and intimacy. Afterwards she shared her own painful experience of childhood sexual abuse. Having learned so much in my friendship with Richard, I was able to hold her for hours in a supervised and secure setting, as she grieved the pain and shame of her childhood abuse. She came to find peace and safety in my arms, and experienced the healing power of healthy touch.

She and I became the best and purest of friends, and many months later, when I was struggling with my own mother issues (who was very critical and a perfectionist), and a lifetime of trying to please others and perform in order to be loved, this wonderful woman provided a safe, unconditional haven of acceptance and support.

I remember feeling so loved, so connected, so close and intimate, that it seemed the most natural next step would have been to be sexual. Yet, there was absolutely no need, no compulsion to go there. She was not my wife, nor I her husband, and I was completely at peace and fulfilled. I felt more deeply than I ever had in my life, that I had separated my deepest desire for love from any misplaced sexual desire, and felt liberated from the needy, lustful desires I had continued to harbor deep within the darkest, most struggling corners of my heart.

At that moment I felt so cleansed, so genuine, and capable of loving, a son of God rather than the little devil that I thought I was, who had everyone fooled. I realized that the "hard on" that I thought I always had was really a "heart on," and the bosom that I was longing for was wrapped up in the nurturing I never experienced in childhood from my mom. I cannot express how liberated I felt at that moment, and how many times in the months and years that followed that authenticity empowered me to cut through the sexual confusion, be fearless in loving, and provide a safe harbor and haven for others in the healing process, as I was for Richard long ago.

I am deeply grateful for my dearest friend's courage and boldness in helping to pioneer the power of healthy touch as an instrument of emotional healing. I am sure that Time, Touch & Talk will help us become more healed and whole, create more genuine and intimate relationships, and make a happier, healthier, more connected and loving world.

—Phillip

HEALING HUMANITY: TIME, TOUCH & TALK

SECTION TWO—TOUCH

Love is the medicine that heals all pain.

Very few people have been able to live freely within the flesh and maintain healthy boundaries—being physically intimate with others without having sex (unless with one's partner). There is no freedom without responsibility. The goal is to create bonding and boundaries, love and limits in all relationships. Men have sex to feel love, and women need love to have sex. *Sex does not equal love. Touch does not equal sex.* We need true intimacy, healthy attachment sans sex, inside and outside of marriage.

> ### Dying from a Compliment
>
> Many years ago I was having dinner in a restaurant with a colleague. Our waitress was dressed seductively—breasts bursting out of her blouse, hair up and falling on her shoulders. I said, "You are so beautiful," and it appeared as if I had deeply insulted her. She was incapable of receiving my compliment because she obviously thought and felt so bad about herself. It was clear that she had a father wound, or perhaps had incurred some abuse by men (the Marilyn Monroe complex), and perhaps acted seductively, seeking men's attention and approval, yet unable to receive the slightest compliment.
>
> To my colleague and me, this young lady had such low self-esteem and an opposite-sex attachment wound. Women who dress seductively often experience father or masculine hunger. Men who lust after women have mother

> hunger, or wounding with women. Lusting after men or women is neither normal nor natural. It is an affectation representing unhealed wounds and unmet loved needs. Again, I am not talking about appreciating the beauty of a man or woman. Art is art. Beauty is beauty. Sexualizing another human being is always unhealthy.
>
> —Richard

It bears repeating once again: *If children do not sufficiently bond with either father and/or mother and other relatives during infancy and early child development, those core needs for bonding become eroticized after adolescence and well into adulthood.* Sex, or exhibiting one's sexuality, then becomes a means whereby the individual is attempting to regain lost love. They need healthy touch, to be held in the bosom of their family and community. The solution is never sex, because the basic needs are primal and that of a child— for attachment, intimacy, understanding: Time, Touch & Talk.

Our bodies somaticize our inner wounds and unmet love needs. We become sick because we long for love. It bears repeating that one of the saddest things in the world is that it's OK to pet dogs, cats, and other animals (pets being a multi-billionaire dollar annual industry), and yet it is inappropriate to hug another person without being suspected of being weird or a pervert! Yes, there are sexual predators. However, the majority of the human race are NOT predators, just hungry souls locked in the cages of their skin. Additionally, it is acceptable for children with Down's Syndrome, who are generally more affectionate, to hug others, even strangers, but it is not acceptable for the rest of us to do so!

SECTION TWO—TOUCH

• •

The Touch Revolution of TTT will begin to turn this sad phenomenon around.

• •

In general, to protect our children from sexual abuse, we teach them not to trust people. We tell teachers to stop hugging their students. *Instead of promoting the solution— teaching about healthy touch and healthy hugs—we promote the problem by enacting legislation that forbids healthy touch. In this way, we are creating potential sex addicts and workaholics—touch-deprived teens and future adults.*

WE NEED TO TEACH HEALTHY TOUCH TO ALL HUMANKIND.

It is possible to diminish the sex, porn, and erotica industries by helping all children, teens, and adults to experience healthy touch on a regular basis. Practice holding and hugging with your family and friends. Touch heals. We have suffered enough abuse, violence, and disasters. The time has come to experience and practice healthy touch daily. Again, twelve hugs per day will keep the doctor away, improve your health, reduce stress, increase productivity, and promote greater happiness.

It starts with one person at a time. YOU CAN MAKE A BIG DIFFERENCE.

• •

*We either learn by blood—accidents, tragedies, death;
or we learn by heart—loving ourselves and others.
Please start hugging today!*

• •

Who will give a healthy, non-sexual hug to a child, teenager, or adult? We pay for massages, haircuts just to feel a bit of touch (oh now, admit it), a hairdresser, chiropractor (I know a handsome chiropractor and women flock to him, not so much for an adjustment, but just to be touched by such a good-looking man!). Twelve hugs a day! Let's do it! *Succeed small rather than fail big.* Start hugging three people per day. Then after one month, increase to five hugs per day. After a few months, increase to eight hugs per day. Continue until you are giving and receiving twelve hugs per day. Keep practicing hugging family, friends, and others in your community (more about this in the Community section).

Masturbation

Sex is a God-given gift, and ideally, best expressed in the security, trust, and safety of a committed marriage. It is an act of love and intimacy. Many faiths have different teachings about masturbation. And many people experience guilt, shame, and anxiety after masturbating, which feeds an already wounded part of the psyche. It becomes an endless cycle of unmet needs, anxiety, masturbation (perhaps combined with porn), guilt/shame, and over and over again. We need to stop the cycle and discover what drives us to do that which we don't want to do. *The cause is more important and more powerful than the effect.*

I want to be clear, I am not making a moral statement about whether masturbation is right or wrong. This is not my intention. Each person decides the benefit, or not, of masturbating. What I am discussing here is *compulsive* masturbation, a habit that may become a deterrent to a fulfilling sexual relationship with one's partner.

Some reasons why we may masturbate:

- To self-soothe: comfort from stress or conflict in present-day relationships.
- As a substitute for intimacy with others. Fantasy and masturbation are easier than creating and/or maintaining real relationships.

- To reward yourself for hard work or a job well done.
- To numb physical or emotional pain.
- Your inner child's way of getting your attention.
- A way to get back into your body. By being a pleaser, one gets disconnected from the true self. Touching yourself and masturbating then becomes a path of re-entry to the soul.
- It has become habitual: physiology of addiction—enough is never enough.

Masturbation may become habitual for some from adolescence. It is a way to take care of oneself when no one else is. It is generally accompanied by sexual fantasies. Those who are pleasers may masturbate as a way of getting dirty, rebellious, and real. By masturbating, *I* regain control of my life.

We need to stop the cycle of guilt and shame. Identify the causes and give ourselves grace. Because many of us were or are pleasers and perfectionists, we may feel guilty and shameful about masturbating. Also, marriage is not a solution for compulsive masturbation and sexual fantasies. Many men continue to masturbate throughout marriage.

A friend of mine, who is a pastoral and couples' counselor, commented on his twenty-years of experience:

"I often met young men, shy, reserved and repressed emotionally, who resorted to a fantasy/porn/masturbation life, assuring themselves that it was a temporary fix from loneliness and their need to satisfy their sexual desire while committed to sexual abstinence before marriage. They were confident that once they had a real sexual partner, they would not need the porn and masturbation, only to find that the habits were hard to break, and easy to fall back on in times of stress, hurt and difficulty in their marriage.

"Women's response to their husband's porn and masturbation habits varies according to their values, self-worth and security in the relationship. I have seen marriages destroyed by the husband's unbreakable habit, and have counseled those who had so trained themselves neurologically to respond to porn (with its dopamine pleasure-reward rush, and the oxytocin a man gets from ejaculation—his biggest dose ever), that they had the heart-rending, shameful experience of being unable to get aroused with their own wives without visualizing porn: imagining other women in debased, violent, and lurid fantasies.

"I have also seen porn-trained husbands demand their partners to be objectified lust objects, with no clue to their wife's needs or how to awaken, arouse, or inspire them sexually." —Phillip

Meanwhile, today there is a new phenomenon called Online Infidelity, where married men are hooking up with new or old love interests. These new and old habits don't disappear without intervention.

Find the causes and create positive alternatives. As a man, if you decrease or stop masturbating, you may experience nocturnal emissions—a natural release when you sleep. This is nature's way of taking care of sperm buildup. Become the CEO of your body. The desire to masturbate is just a part of you. Don't let your body be in control. Find the causes and create positive alternatives.

How to resolve unwanted masturbation:

1. Breathe when you wish to masturbate. Listen to the message from your soul. Embrace your desires. What I mean is to speak to them and discover what is beneath the surface, what is behind those desires. They have a lot to teach you that has little to do with sex. Listen and learn from your body and soul.
2. Forgive yourself if you feel guilty about masturbating, and then...

3. Pray or meditate to identify the cause(s) and/or genuine need(s).
4. Call a friend or accountability partner and share what you are going through.
5. Journal: *Identify the triggers* that led/lead to masturbation and/or unwanted sexual behavior (use the HALT diagnostic tool explained below).
6. Deal effectively with the cause(s):
   a. Resolve conflicts in relationships—make peace with the person you are upset with.
   b. Heal painful emotions—work through it yourself or seek help.
   c. Stop isolating yourself and get your needs met in healthy relationships. Isolation=Death. Give and receive healthy touch.
   d. Reduce stress—create a more balanced life.
7. Create positive alternatives:
   a. Work out, take walks, exercise.
   b. Give to others, volunteer work—direct your energy outward.
   c. Receive healthy touch—massage, healthy hugs, holding.
8. Use inner child dialogue and drawing.

The HALT diagnostic tool is a simple way to identify causes for unwanted masturbation and/or sexual activity.

Hungry: There may be physical hunger which turns into sexual desires. Additionally, feelings of rejection experienced in personal or professional relationships may lead to emotional hungering for or lusting after another person, and resulting in masturbation/porn, sexual hook-ups, or use of substances to self-medicate.

Angry: Unexpressed feelings may become eroticized. When we suppress and then repress our feelings, i.e., anger, frustration, sadness, etc., abracadabra the desire to masturbate or have sex emerges.

Lonely: Legitimate needs for intimacy that go unmet may be experienced as sexual desires. Once again, isolation equals misery/death.

Tired—Stress factors kick in and the desire to take care of oneself by using sexual habits may arise.

For those seeking to resolve compulsive masturbation/porn and unwanted sexual behaviors, I suggest starting and using a Sex Journal on a regular basis. It will help you to understand your inner thoughts, feelings, and needs, and to learn about the triggers that may stimulate unwanted sexual behaviors. A trigger is any activity, event, or situation that will lead one to act out sexually and/or become emotionally distressed.

Journaling helps you achieve some distance from the intensity of the experience. By doing this either before or after you have acted out, soon you will learn what triggers your unwanted behavior. Then you may take positive action steps to resolve the issue, i.e., express your feelings with a sympathetic witness, give and receive healthy touch, volunteer and help others, resolve conflicts with loved ones or co-workers, exercise, etc.

Keep your focus balanced—inward and outward. Once again, there is a danger that during the healing process one may become too introspective. Create joy in your life. Give to others. Keep your energy flowing outward as well as inward. Make sure you exercise, give to others, engage in healthy relationships, experience joy, and play!

While facilitating a support group for ten years, I developed a motto:

• •

Don't reach in, reach out!

• •

The meaning is simple: Instead of masturbating or indulging oneself (in self-pity or self-destructive behaviors), reach out and share with a friend, or find someone in need. Give of yourself to others. Sharing and giving generates energy.

Sexual Fantasies

Believe it or not, most sexual fantasies are not really about sex! Let me say that again: *Sexual fantasies represent unresolved wounds of the past, and unmet needs for love.* No matter how kinky or bizarre your sexual fantasies may be, they hold the keys to your heart.

I have created several therapeutic sexual fantasy exercises that have been extremely effective helping individuals discover and uncover the hidden meaning behind their sexual desires. These exercises helped each man or woman resolve hurts that were totally blocked from consciousness. Perhaps this approach may seem counter-intuitive to you. That maybe I am fostering the problem, rather than focusing on the solution? I assure you, the opposite is true. By going through the presenting "problem," in this case the sexual fantasy, you will arrive at your core truth—hurts in your heart that have not healed, and legitimate needs for love that remain unfulfilled in healthy, healing relationships. And now I present two very effective exercises to help you discover the deeper meaning of your sexual fantasies:

SECTION TWO—TOUCH

1. Play the part of each person in the scene. Stand in his or her shoes, and speak to yourself, if you happen to be the protagonist in the fantasy. If you are not in the fantasy, also play the part of each participant and speak to the main character. Allow each person in the fantasy to share his or her truth to the protagonist. After each person shares, finally step into the role of yourself, or the protagonist. Speak your truth to each person in the fantasy. Perhaps your genitals need to share his or her story as well.

    You may be able to do this by yourself, or you may need a professional therapist or mentor to assist you as there may be profound meaning and hurts that need to be released. Doing this alone may not bring the desired outcome. Once again: What was created in broken relationships must be healed in healthy relationships.

2. Have someone sit across from you. This must be a safe person, someone you trust implicitly with your deepest and darkest secrets. Before you start to share, move your position, either on the sofa or simply move your chair a little to the left or right. When you sit in this new position, you are no longer yourself. You become your sexual fantasy, your deepest, darkest wants, needs, and desires.

    Allow your sexual fantasy to speak. For example, "I want you to come close to me, and begin to unbutton my shirt. Then I want you to start kissing me all over my chest, and licking me with your tongue."

    After you finish sharing a few sentences, switch chairs with your safe person. She or he then becomes your sexual fantasy, and repeats to you what she or he heard, using the same tone and language. You just listen, and take it in. After they finish, switch chairs again.

Then you continue with your fantasy, painting the scene, what unfolds next? "Now you take off my pants, unbuckle my belt, undo the zipper and drop my pants to the ground. Finally, you slide my underwear off."

After you speak a few more lines and desires, then switch positions with the other person again.

She or he will become your sexual fantasy, repeating what you said. Again, each time you listen. Hearing your fantasy spoken is quite affirming. Keep repeating this, going back and forth, until you go deeper and deeper. When you continue this sexual fantasy exercise, which may take anywhere from 30 minutes to over an hour, you will eventually hit bottom, going from sexual fantasy to your core need for genuine love and affection. You may also access core wounds, the origins of your unmet love needs.

You will discover by using either or both of these exercises that your sexual fantasies are not about sex, but hold the keys to unlock your heart and release the pain of your past. If you access your wounds during these exercises, grieve and let it out. If you need to be held, ask your partner to do so. Tears are the medicine to melt the pain and heal our hearts. Of course, you may need to repeat these exercises several or many times before you find the real truth. Your heart may not trust you at first. Just like the inner child healing process, he will only share his deepest thoughts, feelings, and needs when he knows that you will be there to take care of him. Be a good parent to your soul.

SECTION TWO—TOUCH

Family Healing

Infidelity Statistics 2017

- In over 1/3 of marriages, one or both partners admit to cheating.
- 22% of men say that they've cheated on their significant other.
- 14% of women admit to cheating on their significant other.
- 36% of men and women admit to having an affair with a coworker.
- 17% of men and women admit to having an affair with a sister-in-law or brother-in-law.
- People who have cheated before are 350% more likely to cheat again.
- Affairs are most likely to occur two years into a marriage.
- 35% of men and women admit to cheating while on a business trip.
- 9% of men admit they might have an affair to get back at a spouse.
- 14% of women admit they might have an affair to get back at a spouse.
- 10% of affairs begin online.
- 40% of the time, online affairs turn into real life affairs.
- 70% of married women and 54 percent of married men did not know of their spouses' extramarital activity.
- In the United States, 17% of all the divorces that occur are due to adultery on the part of either or both the parties.

Retrieved from: https://www.trustify.info/blog/infidelity-statistics-2017
http://www.divorcestatistics.info/latest-infidelity-statistics-of-usa.html

U.S. high school students surveyed in 2017

- 40% have had sexual intercourse.
- 10% had four or more sexual partners.
- 7% had been physically forced to have sexual intercourse when they did not want to.
- 30% had had sexual intercourse during the previous 3 months, and, of these
    - 46% did not use a condom the last time they had sex.
    - 14% did not use any method to prevent pregnancy.
    - 19% had drunk alcohol or used drugs before last sexual intercourse.
- Nearly 10% of all students have never been tested for human immunodeficiency virus (HIV).
- CDC (Centers for Disease Control) data show that lesbian, gay, and bisexual high school students are at substantial risk for serious health outcomes as compared to their peers.
- Sexual risk behaviors place youth at risk for HIV infection, other sexually transmitted diseases (STDs), and unintended pregnancy.
- Young people (aged 13-24) accounted for an estimated 21% of all new HIV diagnoses in the United States in 2016.
- Among young people (aged 13-24) diagnosed with HIV in 2016, 81% were gay and bisexual males.
- Half of the 20 million new STDs reported each year were among young people, between the ages of 15 to 24.
- Nearly 210,000 babies were born to teen girls aged 15–19 years in 2016.

Retrieved from: https://www.cdc.gov/healthyyouth/sexualbehaviors

Data from September 2011 to September 2015 in interviews with 20,621 men and women, including 4,134 teenagers. The sample is nationally representative:

- More than 42% of never-married adolescents ages 15-19 say they had sex at least once.
- Researchers from the National Center for Health Statistics report that from 2011 to 2015, 42.4% of never-married girls (four million) and 44.2% of never-married boys (4.4 million) had had sexual intercourse.
- More than 35% of girls and almost 28% of boys said that having sex was against their religion or moral code.
- A fifth of both boys and girls cited fear of pregnancy as the reason for abstaining. Almost 23% said they had not yet found the right person.

Retrieved from: https://www.nytimes.com/2017/06/26/health/united-states-teenagers-sexual-activity.html

Parents, please regularly hug and hold your children. Teenagers are having sex earlier and more often than ever before. Why? Of course the entertainment industry and media promote sex. However, the greatest reasons are the 6 Ds: divorce, dysfunctional families, digital technology, divided communities/racial barriers, decline of morals/values, and daycare (read more about the 6 Ds below).

Healthy touch within the family is a natural remedy for the 6 Ds which are dismantling our communities and culture. When you wake up in the morning, greet your partner and children with a warm hug and a kiss. I'm a Jewish man and we are a very hugging and kissing people. My wife and I continue to hug and kiss our adult children. We kiss on the lips! In many cultures this is the norm.

Here in the West, because of the Puritan heritage (remember, publicly puritans and privately perverts), touch became associated with the notion of sex. It is time to blow up that fallacious concept. Hug and kiss your children in the morning before they leave for school, upon their return, and before they go to bed at night (minimum of three hugs and kisses per day). If they are very young, hold them in your arms at night. Listen to their stories from the daytime. Reattach with your children in the evening if you work during the day, or if they are either in school or childcare.

The more healthy touch and attention you provide, the less they will need to masturbate, look at Internet porn, and hook up with sexual partners. Additionally, practice good listening and sharing skills taught in the final section of this book. Of course, parental relationships are of the utmost importance for the health and wellbeing of their family. Resolving personal and relational issues are key for securely attached children. Healthy touch and securely attached children = happy and fulfilled adolescents and adults.

Teachers are the second parents for our children. They educate our kids, spending approximately six-to-eight hours per day molding their hearts and minds. It is totally natural for teachers to hug our children. Of course, the school system must do thorough

background checks on all teachers and staff to make sure they are not sex offenders. We certainly need to protect our children from wounded men and women. *Once again, instead of legislating the problem, we need to encourage the solution.* It should be appropriate for teachers to hug their students, our children.

While on this subject, one of my best friends was incarcerated for ten years for sexually abusing his children. What he did was deplorable. However, putting these men away without rehabilitation is another travesty. There is hope and help for these wounded souls. You may be shocked at such a suggestion, thinking, "They should be locked away for good to protect our children." If only it were that simple, but alas, it is not so. One of my favorite professors in graduate school taught us: When in the room with both the perpetrator and victim, always be confused. Why? Because every perpetrator was once a victim of childhood sexual abuse, always and in every case. She had worked over 25 years for the Department of Social Services in Seattle, Washington. We must help these wounded souls heal at the root of their core wounds, and assist them in fulfilling basic unmet love needs—again, every perpetrator was also a victim of childhood sexual abuse. It does not excuse their horrific behaviors, and they too need our love. I know well, because I am a survivor of childhood sexual abuse.

Six Ds Dismantling Our World Today

- Divorce
- Daycare
- Digital technology
- Dysfunctional families
- Division
- Decline of morals/values

The 6 Ds are wreaking havoc upon our present and future generations:

Divorce: About forty to fifty percent of marriages in the USA end in divorce. As mentioned, parents are in the position of Mr. & Mrs. God, representing the masculine and feminine nature of our Creator. If parents separate and divorce regardless of the child's age, it fractures their inner world. Just do a simple Internet search and read the long-term ramifications of divorce upon children.

Daycare: My mentor, Dr. Martha Welch, commented that daycare is singlehandedly creating detached children who have difficulty reconnecting with their parents each evening. She said unless parents hold their children each night, they will develop attachment strains and seek unhealthy means to soothe their unmet needs.

Digital technology: Technological devices are oftentimes replacing real relationships. Reaching out and touching someone cannot be accomplished online. Only human skin touch soothes our souls and creates well-adjusted children and future adults. It is becoming the norm to see two people out together at a coffee shop or restaurant where one or both are on their cell phones and not speaking to each other. Digital technology is creating a generation of detached men and women.

Dysfunctional families: Sadly, this is the new norm; just watch many prime-time television shows. Affairs, divorce, parents disconnected from each other and their wounded children lead to maladjusted behaviors. Sex becomes a substitute for love. Violence and addictions are increasing. When I was doing my internship at a mental health agency while in graduate school, there was a cartoon on the bulletin board that read, "Adult Children of Normal Families." Pictured was a large auditorium with one person sitting in the front row, and one person sitting in the back row. The rest of the seats were vacant! That says it all.

Division: The differences between religions, races, sexual orientations, to name just a few, are creating barriers that lock us away from anyone or anything that appears different from us. Instead of breaking down the walls that divide us, we are erecting new ones.

Decline of moral values: Abandoning our morals, ethics, and values has been the downfall of one great empire after another throughout human history. Morally confused and secular-humanistic children easily become promiscuous adults. When we discard our moral compass, relativism reigns and anything goes.

These 6 Ds are resulting in the rise of addictions, sexual activity (porn, Internet sex, romance novels/erotica, affairs, multiple partners), looking for love in all the wrong places, and in all the wrong ways. This applies to children, teens, and adults. These coping behaviors never last. Let me reiterate once again, our real need is to bond, belong, and connect. Many "hook up with another person" to feel skin touch, to gain a sense of connection, even for a moment.

Before implementing any new parenting skill, or change in your family culture, sit together with your children and explain what is going to occur. Allow them to ask questions and respond honestly from your heart. Let them know that you may not have done any of these things in the past, but now you have learned new skills to create greater love and intimacy in your family.

Exercises for Healthy Touch in Families

- Hug and kiss your children: 1) in the morning, 2) when they or you return home, and 3) before bed.
- Walk together hand-in-hand with your children. In many Asian and Middle Eastern cultures, it is normal for friends of the same sex to walk down the street holding hands. It is the most natural thing. In the West, once again people assume that if two people of the same sex walk hand-in-hand, they must be "gay." Actually, heterosexual women can get away with this. By the way, I have and continue to do this with my two adult sons on occasion, and of course our daughter as well. First break all the rules! We are here to expand love, not follow norms that prohibit the growth and healing of humanity.
- As parents, walk hand-in-hand with your children, regardless of their age. You will always be their father or mother. Walk hand-in-hand with your grandparents, grandchildren, relatives, family members, and friends.
- Hold hands, face each other, establish eye contact, and express your emotions (sad, mad, glad, afraid, love).
- Use the Feelings Wheel, provided in the Self-Healing section of Time, to begin a new culture of expressing your emotions and feelings with close family and friends. Then

SECTION TWO—TOUCH

add the gift of healthy touch. Face each other, look into one another's eyes, hold hands, and each one share how she or he is feeling at the moment. Regular practice of sharing one's feelings while holding hands and establishing eye contact will become as natural as speaking and listening (the next topic to be shared in the Talk section).

SECTION TWO—TOUCH

- Spoon or cuddle with your partner.

Cuddling or spooning one's partner does not need to be sexual in nature. It is a moment of full body contact without any need for sex. As mentioned in the previous section, both partners lay together naked, breathe together, give and receive the gift of healthy touch. Men need to learn physical touch without sex. Practice two times per week, holding for five to ten minutes without clothes. Do this for one month, then increase to naked holding/cuddling three times per week for ten minutes. NO SEX after you cuddle or spoon naked. Keep cuddling and sex separate. This discipline will allow you to become more giving and loving. Remember the penile principle: it's just blood in a shaft, and what goes up will come down. Practice healthy touch without sex. This will increase intimacy and satiate your essential need for skin touch. Health will increase, productivity will increase, and intimacy will be a natural byproduct of holding without sex. And by all means please make love with your partner! Just keep naked holding/cuddling and sexual activity separate.

Wrap your arms around the waist of your partner, while your chest is against his or her back. This may be done anywhere in the house, with clothes on!

This is a wonderful gift to share with your partner—putting your arms around him or her from the back. This is a warm, affectionate hug of reassurance and intimacy. The partner receiving may put her or his hands on the hands of the other. Be sure to switch it up. The man holds his wife, and sometimes the wife holds her husband. It is an extremely supportive gesture of love.

One caution: If one partner has experienced childhood sexual or physical abuse, this form of holding and touch needs to be discussed to make it safe for her or him. If one partner comes from behind the other to initiate this form of holding, it may shock and frighten him or her. Therefore, first discuss this with your partner. It is important that both feel safe, seen, and understood.

- Massage one another.

There are many types of massage that may be exchanged between partners: full body massage, shoulder massage, foot massage, or hand massage. There are many books on massaging your partner. Exchange. Because of our busy schedules, you may need to make appointments to massage each other. Even a simple five to ten-minute massage is an incredible gift to both give and receive. Start by doing this one time per week, or one time every two weeks. *Succeed small rather than fail big.* Make simple, measurable commitments, and feel good when you accomplish those. Then you may increase the number of times you exchange a massage. Perhaps one week he massages her, and the next week she massages him.

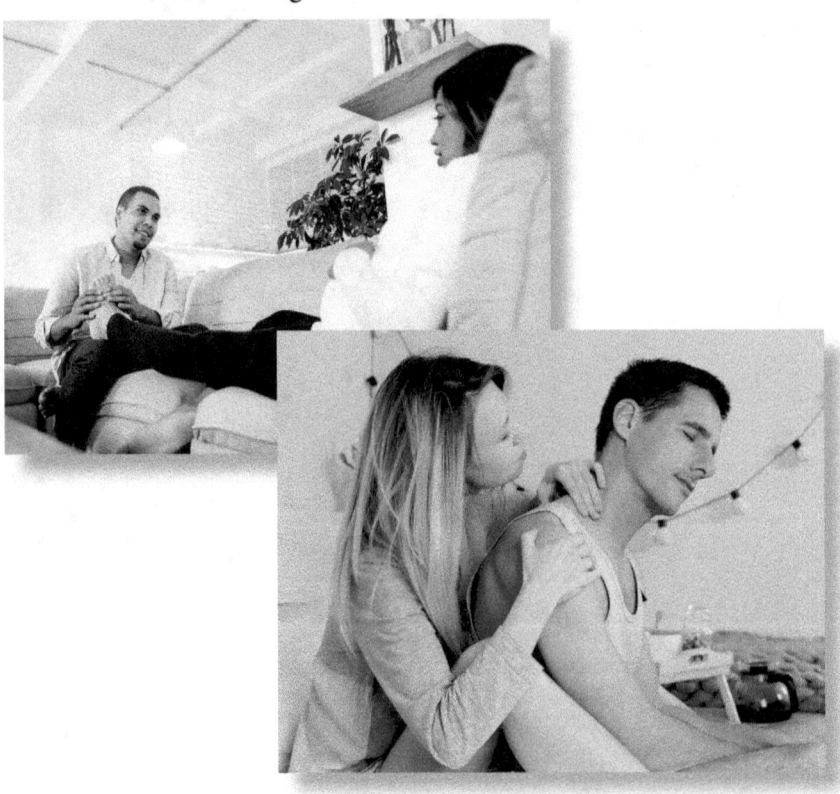

- Gently, hold the cheeks of your child or spouse with the palms of your hands and look into each other's eyes.

    This gentle caressing of his or her cheeks is a way to express your love and affection. It also calms the physiology of the other person. Establish eye contact while you hold her or his cheeks. Communicate affection with your eyes, and then with your words. "I love you just the way you are." "You mean the world to me."

- Hug your spouse and kiss her or him before you depart for work each day.

    Say, "I love you" while looking into her or his eyes. Do the same with each one of your children—hug, kiss, eye contact and say, "I love you."
- Display affection in front your children.

    Hug and kiss, hold hands, put your arm around her or his shoulders while watching TV—modeling Mr. & Mrs. God loving each other.
- Sandwich hugs.

This is a fun hug: Father and mother are the bread, and your child is the meat. Father stands on one side and mother stands on the other, while the child is in the middle. You sandwich your son or daughter and give them a beautiful hug and sense of security. It is a wonderful feeling to be sandwiched by love!

Fathers, please hug your adolescent daughters! Be close to her. Put your arms around her. She needs healthy touch from Dad, uncles, brothers, and grandfathers. She needs to incorporate the masculine into her inner psyche through this stage of development. Otherwise, she will spend the rest of her life seeking your love in the arms of other men; searching for father's love the rest of her life, and making her husband and other men hostage to a hurt, rejected, abandoned little girl—this is part of the unconscious marriage (read more about this phenomena in Harville

Hendrix's *Getting the Love You Want*). Additionally, her sons will be damaged as she may unconsciously require them to take care of her unmet needs for masculine attention and affection.

Daughters need to internalize their father's/uncle's/grandfather's/older brother's love and affection. In this way they will experience being valued, cherished, feminine, and loved.

Sons need the exact same love from their mothers, grandmothers, aunts, and sisters during adolescence. They need to feel the admiration and appreciation from women, affirming their masculinity. "You are strong. I admire you as a young man."

Single mothers and single fathers need lots of touch, as well as their children. Places of worship would be wise to assign a family to embrace single parents and their children. Otherwise, these children will be susceptible to addictions, gang activity, sexual and gender confusion, violence, etc. Please hug a single parent and her or his child or children today!

Community Healing

Touch in the workplace is an extremely touchy subject. There are strict guidelines to prevent sexual harassment, which is a good thing. We have made lots of progress to avert unsuitable behavior. But once again, we may be throwing out the baby with the bathwater by legislating the problem and not promoting the solution. Inappropriate sexual behavior or advances are wrong one hundred percent of the time. However, let's begin to promote healthy touch in families, schools, places of worship, and in the work place. Stopping sexual misconduct and harassment is the beginning, not the end. The next step is to begin teaching appropriate touch between colleagues and co-workers.

Once again, Hollywood moguls, movie stars, politicians, and religious leaders are being outed daily for sexual misconduct. The MeToo# and TimesUp# movements have now spread around the world. Men and women are standing up against sexual abuse and sexual harassment. This is step one. Who is promoting the next step? Who has the answers to really stop this epidemic of sexual abuse and misconduct? TTT does. It is time to provide solutions for touch deprived and touch starved men and women, regardless of their station in life. Just the other day a friend of mine saw his colleague, a man in his early 70s, coming onto a woman. Knowing this man's family background and history of womanizing, he commented, "It was so obvious his inner child was hungering for his mother's love."

Many of us, knowing or unknowingly, use surrogates to provide the parental touch we crave: barbers, beauticians, bar tenders, doctors, and masseurs. They nurture us because we are hungry for attention, affection, and connection. Of course others turn to alcohol, drugs, gambling, food, Internet porn, masturbation, romance novels, erotica, and hooking up for anonymous sexual encounters. If only these lasted and worked. But our deeper needs for healthy touch and real connection are often ignored.

Reach out and touch someone—start a touch program in your family, place of worship, club, school, and business. I am a member of my local Toastmasters International club, an excellent venue to improve one's public speaking and leadership skills. I gave several speeches on TTT and had every club member stand to give and receive healthy hugs. When I attend our bi-weekly groups, I give and receive many hugs with our club members. You may do the same in your family, local organizations, places of worship, and by all means, educate people at work.

The flames of hatred may be extinguished through healthy touch—healing the world one hug at a time. This is my heart's desire. I can see it now. No more terrorists. No more Israelis and Palestinians killing one another. No more men and women of power falling so far from grace. No more employees being subject to sexual harassment. No more students being bullied. Teaching healthy touch is the antidote to sexual misconduct.

How can we kill someone that we are holding in our arms? We are all family and we do not need war and tragedy any longer to bring us together. Why should more than three billion people, nearly half the world's population, live in poverty when there are more than enough natural resources for everyone to share equally? Healthy touch can start a process of reconciliation that can end the wars, heal the world, and recreate a caring global family.

In churches, synagogues, mosques, or temples, people shake hands or don't touch at all. Why not hug? Shouldn't our houses of worship be the safest places on earth and therefore sanctuaries for healthy touch? In every church I attended, I initiated a hugging program. What a wonderful place to demonstrate healthy touch. The house of God should be a place where anyone may experience healthy touch without fear of sexual harassment, misconduct, or misinterpretation. This must include Catholic, Christian, Jewish. Muslim, Hindu, and other places of worship worldwide. If only this might be…which is the goal of TTT.

Speak to the leader of your place of worship about starting a healing touch program. Introduce him or her to this TTT book. Show him or her photos and suggest beginning healthy hugs today. Wouldn't it be wonderful while attending a service on Sunday, or whatever day you worship, to experience healthy hugs from those around you? Now that would be something to look forward to each week!

A word of caution: I've heard from many women in different places of worship, "When a man hugs me, he puts his hand on my butt! I feel so violated." Men, never, ever put your hand on a woman's butt unless she is your wife and you have her permission. Once again, healthy hugs are one arm above the other person's shoulder, and one arm below. Place your hands on the other person's back, never on their butt.

We must also learn to hug those of the same sex, men hugging other men, and women hugging other women. There is often fear of hugging someone of the same sex, "Oh, you're gay!" or "Maybe they'll think I'm gay!" No, it isn't necessarily so. It is both healthy and healing to hug those of the same sex. It is normal, natural, and necessary to the process of developing healthy children, adolescents, and adults. We must learn to embrace both genders, and please, no pats on the back, A-frame, or duck hugs.

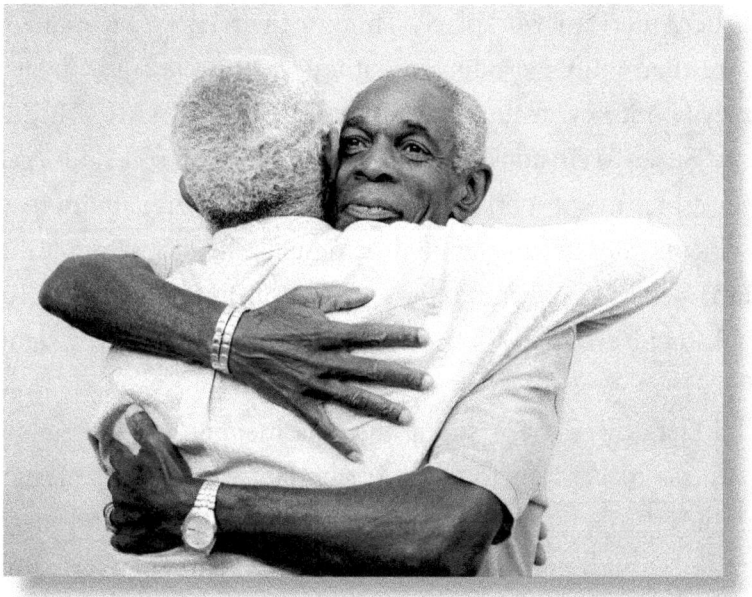

When was the last time someone touched you (other than sex)? We all carry skin hunger. The world is touch deprived. Can you imagine if we give and receive twelve healthy hugs per day? What radical changes might occur? Viewing Internet porn would decrease. Sexual hook-ups would decrease. Affairs outside of marriage would decrease. Public figures falling from grace would decrease. Perpetrators hurting children would decrease. Wars would decrease. Hatred among family members would decrease.

• •

We are all hungry for healthy touch!

• •

TOUCH ≠ SEX

The Treasure of Elders

"You have an aging workforce," says economist Sophia Koropeckyj of Moody's Analytics. "Older workers are changing the dynamics of the American workplace. Though their knowledge and skills make many more productive, others may be less adaptable and savvy about new technology," Koropeckyj says. AARP Vice President Susan Weinstock says older workers bring soft skills "gained over a lifetime of work, like calm under pressure, ability to solve problems, ability to listen and be empathetic. These are uniquely human skills that a computer or robot can't replace" (USA Today, Paul Davidson, "Baby boomers keep pushing job growth," January 10, 2019, page 2).

Elders carry the wisdom of a lifetime, and hold generational treasures to pass on to their descendants. They may bless their families through their healthy touch of children, adolescents, and adults. Multigenerational Housing projects in the UK, Germany and other European countries are creating opportunities for the elderly to interact with kindergarten and elementary school children. All are being blessed and the benefits are staggeringly wonderful. The elders have a purpose for life, and the youth are receiving love, attention, education, and affection. (Retrieved from: https://www.theguardian.com/world/2014/may/02/germany-multigeneration-house-solve-problems-britain).

Elders need to be reinstated into their rightful place within the family and community at large. Instead of relegating them to old-age homes, let us bring them back into the bosom of our families. Having our parents and grandparents live with us will bless our children, grandchildren, and future generations. Separate living is such a wasted opportunity for continued growth, healing, and love for everyone. Let us respect, regard, and restore our elders to their rightful place as the leaders of our families.

Exercise

Here is a simple yet profound exercise that you may facilitate or initiate in your place of worship. It is a powerful tool to bring healing for men and women in your community. During the exercise, play beautiful, healing music in the background.

1. Women stand in the center of the circle, while men stand behind them and gently put their hands on their shoulders. Exchange names.
2. Each man prays for the woman:
   a. Repent for any wrongdoing that you have committed against any woman.
   b. Pray for the woman in front of you, for her healing, and then give her your blessing.
   c. Pray that she may receive healthy touch from men—receiving and giving.
3. Reverse: Men stand in the center of the circle, while women stand behind them and gently put their hands on their shoulders. Exchange names.
   a. Repent for any wrongdoing that you committed against any man.
   b. Pray for the man in front of you, for his healing, and then give him your blessing.
   c. Pray that he may receive healthy touch from women—receiving and giving.

After you finish, have everyone sit down, and let each man and woman share their experience with one another. After you give each couple sufficient time to express themselves, ask for volunteers to share with the group how it was for her or him. Be sure to have plenty of tissues on hand!

Sexuality on a Spectrum

We do not always know why we are attracted to men or women of the same or opposite sex. We may develop crushes on people of the same-sex or opposite-sex in our lifetime. Many of these may be healthy and natural. However, if early bonding needs from infancy and early childhood with our parents, primary caregivers, and/or peers remained incomplete, then during adolescence, those basic unmet love needs may be experienced as sexual desires and become eroticized.

Because of cultural taboos, we are then prevented from fulfilling the unmet love needs in healthy, non-sexual relationships, and therefore act out sexually to fulfill these early bonding needs for love. Once again, the Puritanical heritage taught us that TOUCH = SEX. This prevents healing and fulfilling basic love needs. The sexual attractions, infatuations, and emotional crushes we experience are messages from the soul—the psyche's attempt to get our attention. "I need love. I need mentoring. I need healthy, healing touch and secure attachment with a male or female figure. I want to be known and to know the other." This is the need of a child, adolescent or young adult. This confusion may continue throughout one's life until hurts of the heart are healed, and basic love needs fulfilled. Again, when sex enters into a relationship as a result of one's sexual or gender confusion, unmet love needs will remain unfulfilled because they are those of a child, and children do not want or need sex.

Today there are so many man-made labels regarding a person's sexuality, sexual or gender identity, sexual preference or orientation. Facebook lists over seventy categories for an individual to define his or her sexual or gender identity. These man-made terms ignore our simple biology—men and women fit perfectly together. Zeno, an ancient Greek philosopher, stated, "The goal of life is living in agreement with nature."

Offering Free Hugs

Begin offering free hugs in local parks, on university campuses, at places of worship before and after the service, outside the post office on the final day of tax returns! All you need to do is make a sign that says, "Free Hugs." Get some friends to assist. Together offer the gift of healthy hugs to those walking by, anyone in need of a hug.

I suggested the Free Hugs idea to many of my Tender, Loving, and Caring (TLC) healing seminar participants over the past decades. In April 2004, a young man who had participated in a recent TLC healing seminar returned to New York City and began a Free Hugs campaign in Washington Square Park in the East Village. He and his friend created FREE HUGS signs and T-shirts and began hugging many who were passing by.

Here are his words after their first event: "Our FREE HUGS was a huge success. We ended up spending most of the day until it rained. We must have given around 200 whopping hugs to people. They complimented us saying Great Huggers! I was amazed at the reception of people. Sure, many thought that we were freaks, but so many people were so welcoming. Whomever wouldn't hug us, we told to hug someone else. We hugged gays, straights, blacks, whites, transgender, and people from around the world. European tourists were the most receptive. It was an awesome experience! We hope to do it again next Sunday."

After a few more Sundays in the park offering Free Hugs, he was interviewed by media from the USA, England, Germany, France, Israel, Poland, and Taiwanese TV stations. They asked him if he had a copyright on the FREE HUGS campaign to which he replied, "I have no copyright on any of what I am doing. I hope that people around the world go out and copy me!" On May 10, 2004 Andrea Elliott of The New York Times wrote an article about this young man's Free Hugs campaign entitled "Inviting the Public's Embrace, One by One." Soon after that he was invited to many European festivals to introduce the FREE HUGS campaign.

Since then, the FREE HUGS idea has taken off around the world. Another young man known as Juan Mann of Sydney, Australia began Free Hugs at the end of June 2004 (just a month later). His story too was picked up by the media, and Free Hugs traveled around the world. Please begin a FREE HUG campaign in your community. Just make some signs and ask some friends to join you. Healthy touch heals the hungry soul!

We have "Happy Hours" in bars. How about a "Happy Hour" with Free Hugs! Start one in your community. Get volunteers, hug each other, and teach the community how to make love, not war! Start Free Hugs groups on Meetup or other social media platforms. It is such a simple idea whose time has come. Actress Olivia Wilde wrote and directed a cute film entitled *Free Hugs*. Healing the World through the Power of Healthy Touch, one hug at a time!

• •

Every behavior is either an expression of love
or a cry for love.

• •

Hug a new person each day. If you are a politician, you may initiate a "Hugging Day" for your town, city or state. How about a

SECTION TWO—TOUCH

FREE HUGS can be done anywhere by anyone. Hugs improve health and overall well-being.

© Richard Cohen, M.A., 2019

"National Hugging Day?" Sounds farfetched, right? But every new idea was once considered impossible. Teens need lots of healthy hugs from their parents, relatives, teachers, and mentors, or they will sexualize this need. They are going through radical hormonal changes in their bodies and brains, and therefore require healthy touch to help them navigate through this tumultuous time in their lives. They will either receive healthy touch or sexualize the need. We decide…

Section Three—Talk

TALK, or good communication, is the Air for all personal and professional relationships, and includes both listening and sharing. Without air, good communication, all relationships will be smothered and die. We need to learn the art of effectively sharing our thoughts, feelings, and needs. Perhaps more important is to learn the art of listening, which takes twice as much energy as it does to share. Remember, we have two ears and one mouth, so we need to listen twice as much as we speak. We must learn about and honor each other's differences: temperament, personality styles, love languages, gender differences, cultural backgrounds, etc.

• •

*Blessed are the flexible and informed,
for they shall not be bent out of shape!*

• •

TALK

Self-Healing
- Effective Listening
- Effective Sharing

Family Healing
- Temperaments
- Personality Types
- Love Languages
- Birth Order
- Gender Differences

Community Healing
- Compassion
- Honoring Differences

Self-Healing

Good communication is like oxygen for all relationships. Without sharing our thoughts, feelings, and needs effectively, there is no possibility for real intimacy and love.

Because we all have different temperaments, characters, and personalities, conflict is inevitable, and is the price we pay for intimacy. I will share more about the differences between temperament, character, and personality in the Family section. Relationships move through three basic stages:

1. Superficial communication: Each one stands on one leg, wearing masks and putting their best foot forward, hence, a two-legged relationship. She brings out the best in him, and he in her. Everyone is showing their best and hiding their worst!

2. Chaos through conflict: Messy middle of the relationship when the masks come down, and the shadows come out. "You're not who I thought you were!" Many wives now try to "change" their husbands to make them what they need or want them to be. Many husbands shut down, and escape through different methods, i.e., overworking, masturbation and porn, affairs. At last, they must either deal with their individual issues, or split up. Now they stand on three legs; sometimes she's more adult-like, other times he may be.

3. Self-awareness and mutual respect: At last the couple stands on four legs. He is aware of his issues and takes responsibility not to project them onto her. She learns proper self-care, not leaning on him to make her feel good about herself. Intimacy and maturity in a relationship occurs when each partner is able to own their issues, honor their differences, and meet each other's needs.

With that in mind, I'm going to share some helpful communication skills. In order to develop the art of effective listening and speaking, practice these exercises often until they become part of your normal conversations. In this way, you will become more powerful and achieve greater intimacy in all personal and professional relationships.

Communication Skills—Effective Listening

1. **Maintain eye contact:** When standing or sitting across from another person, be sure to look her straight in the eyes. This creates your first connection, and lets her know that you are attentive to what she is saying.

2. **Join together.** Rather than give advice or your opinion, stand in her shoes. As you listen, seek to understand her viewpoint. This will take practice as you need to quiet your own thoughts and opinions. Join in her world.

3. **Observe.** Take note of her body language, tone, and words. Research has shown that body language and tone generally say more than the spoken word. Observe her posture, her gestures, and her facial expressions. Are her arms crossed around her chest, or relaxed at her side? Is her face joyful or upset? Listen to the tone of her voice. Is she saying one thing and yet speaking another message through her tone and with her body language? Listen with your eyes, your mind, and your heart.

4. **Practicing reflective listening:**

As suggested by Dr. Harville Hendrix, here is a threefold technique to teach the art of reflective listening:

> *First:* Mirror or paraphrase his communication. After listening to a few sentences, you may say,

"If I heard you correctly, you said that you were upset that I do not greet you with a hug and a kiss when you come home from work. Did I get it? Is there more?"

Continue to listen and paraphrase, listen and paraphrase every few sentences. If he goes on for too long, gently interrupt and say, "Dear, if I heard you correctly, you said..." If you get something wrong, or forget something, don't worry, he will correct you. After his sharing is complete, then summarize all that he spoke:

"In summary, what I heard you say was that you get upset if I don't hug and kiss you when you come home from work. You really need that each night because you work very hard to provide for our family. All you need is for me to honor you in this way. Then you will feel so much better and loved. Is that the essence? Did I get it right?"

If he says, "Yes, but you forgot ..." Then after he finishes, paraphrase this thought and say, "Is that it?" When he says, "Yes," then you move to the next phase.

Please do not put your thoughts, feelings, or inflection into the communication when you paraphrase. It is fine to 100% disagree with the speaker. However, you need to *join* with him and reflect what you heard. In this way, he will feel understood and respected.

Second: Validate his thoughts. Here you imagine how he is thinking based upon what you just heard. It is difficult to separate thoughts and feelings; do your best.

"You make sense to me because you worked hard all day to take care of us and simply want me to validate you with affection. Is that it? Did I get it?"

Here you have to imagine how he *thinks*. You are validating his thoughts. After you finish say, "Is that right?" If it's wrong, don't worry; he will correct you. Then paraphrase what he says and ask, "Is that right?"

If he affirms your understanding of his thinking, then you finish with:

Third: Empathize with his feelings, using simple feeling words (you may refer to the Feelings Wheel).

"Given all that, I imagine you feel hurt, frustrated, and sad. Are those your feelings?"

Wait for him to confirm or amend your suggested simple feeling words.

"Yes, but I also felt upset and mad."

Finish with validating his new feeling words. "I see, you also felt upset and mad. Is that it?" "Yes, thank you for listening and understanding me. I appreciate you very much." You have successfully heard what he was saying.

During reflective listening, you do not have to agree with what the speaker is saying. The important thing is to hear and validate him. Most of the time, we do not need advice; we just need to be heard. When you are paraphrasing, make sure *not* to interject with a sarcastic tone. As best as you can, use the same tone as the speaker. If you use a sarcastic tone, this will invalidate everything he shared. Remember, you don't need to agree, just listen and paraphrase. This takes a lot of practice and patience. As one of my clients brilliantly stated, "I would rather be in relationship than be right."

Reflective listening is learning to walk in the other person's shoes, seeing life through his eyes. And, if you wish to respond to what he just shared, you must ask his permission when you finish the three-step reflective listening process. "Would you like to hear my thoughts?" If he says "Yes," proceed. If he says, "No," then that's it. The communication loop is complete.

5. **Use the magic words**: "Thank you, (person's name), tell me more." If you are too upset by his words, and you cannot paraphrase what he is saying, then simply say, "Thank you (his name), tell me more." This is such a simple, yet effective listening skill. Try it and you will see how great it works with family, friends, co-workers, and your boss.

6. **If all else fails, KYMS**: Keep Your Mouth Shut and just listen without comment. Be a silent witness. You can always add, "Thank you, tell me more." Use KYMS when temperatures are hot, especially yours!

7. **Silence is golden**: Silence is one of the greatest gifts you can give another person. You do not need to fill the empty moments with words or questions. Just "be" with her. It will allow her to know that you are "there" for her, and it gives her the opportunity to go deeper.

8. **Don't look at your watch while she is talking:** Do it when you are speaking.

9. **Mental filters**: People who remain unhealed and/or have not resolved many of their personal issues, continue to project onto others their perceptions, and often, misperceptions. This is very difficult for the listener. For example, I recently left a support group that I attended for eight years. I shared that I had found another group which was more beneficial for me, and had nothing to do with them.

The final day of my participation several of the men in the group attacked me, shouting a list of their grievances. When I turned the volume down (in my mind), and looked into their eyes, I saw hurt little boys who felt abandoned (their mental filters and projections). Arguing and trying to convey my real sentiment would have failed in this situation, when another person is blaming and has age-regressed to past memories. Therefore, in these situations I highly suggest either removing yourself graciously from the conversation, use reflective listening, or KYMS. You cannot change anyone but yourself.

PRACTICE, PRACTICE, PRACTICE, especially during good times. Then when conversations become more heated, you will be able to diffuse the situation by using these effective listening skills.

Communication Skills—Effective Sharing

1. **Use "I" statements, not "You" statements:**

    Own your thoughts, feelings, and needs.
    Do not say: "You shouldn't speak to me that way."
    Say: "I don't like it when you speak to me that way."
    Speak in the first person…
    Do not say: "You upset me when you did…"
    Say: "I get upset when you…"

    Important use of "I" statements: In the USA, we are taught from elementary school to speak in the second person, that it is selfish to begin sentences with "I think…" or "I believe…" or "I feel…" We are also taught to write in a similar manner.

    Listen to the news every evening, or an interview with a celebrity or politician, or someone who just experienced loss. Here are several real-life examples of what you may hear: "You get hurt, and you just don't know what to do. You are beside yourself with fear." "You win an Oscar and you are so surprised." "You heard that a neighbor was killed, and you are so shocked."

Once again, we are taught to speak and write in the second person. This disconnects us from our somatic experiences—our own thoughts, feelings, and needs. Therefore, please begin to shift your awareness to speaking and writing in the first person. For example, "I was very hurt when I heard that my neighbor was killed. It shocked me. I am so sad." "I won the Oscar! I was genuinely surprised." "I got hurt and didn't know what to do."

Each time you use an "I" statement instead of "You" statements when referring to your own experience, you step into your personal power and begin to know thyself more intimately. Begin to listen to yourself when you are sharing with others. Soon you will become aware of when you are speaking in the second person, "You" instead of "I." Slowly change and own your thoughts, feelings, and needs. "I think…" "I feel…" I need…" This is not selfish, but self-full. You are becoming a more powerful man or woman.

2. Practice optimum effective communication:

   a. Eye contact.
   b. Physical touch—with family, friends, and other close relationships.
   c. Responsible language—"I" statements, not "You" statements.

If you have something negative or sad to tell someone, hold his or her hands. This acts as a grounding conduit between you and the other person. Three optimum ways to communicate are with the eyes, words, and touch (holding hands, hands on her shoulders, etc.). Women in business can use this principle to their advantage when they want to close a deal. By touching a man on his shoulder, arm, or hand while saying, "Please buy my (product name)," their message will be that much more convincing.

3. **Encourage conflict resolution:**

Here is a five-step protocol to express your thoughts, feelings, and needs when you are upset about what someone said or did (modified from *Nonviolent Communication* by Marshall B. Rosenberg, Ph.D., and Mankind Project clearing protocol):

First: Present the facts—what he said or did that caused you to have a strong reaction. Make it specific to this one event. Please do *not* say "You always…" or "You never…" or "Everybody says…" or "Everybody thinks…" Keep it focused on this one-time event, what he said or did. Example: "This morning before you left for work, you got angry and yelled at me."

Second: Acknowledge your feelings—use simple feeling words (sad, mad, glad, afraid, etc.). Example: "When you raised your voice to me this morning, I felt scared, mad, and upset."

Third: Identify the judgments and beliefs that you have about what he said or did. Here you also own your projections and personal issues, how what he said or did reminds you of past issues. Example: "When you raise your voice with me, it reminds me of my father's angry outbursts. I become like a naughty little girl."

Fourth: State your needs, desires, or wishes. Example: "I do not deserve to be spoken to in such a manner. When you are upset, would you please speak to me in a civil tone, or ask me to hold you so that I may comfort you. I appreciate that very much."

Fifth: State what you are willing to give to make the relationship work. Example: "I know that I can get upset and lose my temper as well. Therefore, let's both commit to not taking our feelings out on each other. I will ask you to hold me when I'm upset, or I will withdraw from the room to calm down. Please agree to do the same. Thank you."

Be mindful *not* to preach in the third step. No sermons on the sofa. Own your reactions to what he said or did. Make simple requests and offer the same. This conflict resolution protocol works in all personal and professional relationships. Like all communication skills, it takes lots of practice. Try using this and the other skills when things are going well, so when tempers are hot, you will be able to use it more easily.

For those who believe in Christ, he spoke of another conflict resolution protocol written about in Matthew 18:15-18. If you feel hurt by another…

1. Go to him and express your concerns (using good communication skills). If he listens and responds well, great, it's finished. However, if he is defensive and unresponsive…

2. Go to him once again, this time with one or two witnesses so that every matter may be testified as fact. If he apologizes, the matter is settled. If he still remains intractable…

3. Bring the matter to the "church," or a respected body of elders. If he listens and apologizes, finished. If he remains obstinate and unrepentant, then he is to be ignored. Wipe the dust off your feet and move on. You cannot make another person do anything that he is unwilling to do. You can only change yourself.

4. **Learn the 'Sandwich Technique':**

   First: State how you feel about the relationship.
   "I really care about you."
   "I love you."
   "I value our relationship."

Second: State the difficulty that you have with the individual. State what outcome you would like to see.

"Recently, you have been screaming at me a lot. That hurts me deeply. I feel unloved, unimportant, and rejected. I think you are under a lot of pressure, and I'm taking the blame for your frustrations. Please deal with your feelings more responsibly. Do not take them out on me. I am willing to help you in a positive way, but not be your punching bag."

Third: State once again how you feel about the relationship.

"I love you and I am committed to our relationship."

In this way, you sandwich the problem (meat of the sandwich) in between your real feelings of love (the bread). It makes it easier for the other person to receive your sharing. Again, please be responsible in all communication, using "I" statements instead of "You" statements. "I" statements mean that I take responsibility for how I think, feel, and what I need. "You" statements try to make others responsible for your wellbeing.

• •

It is not the situation or person that upsets us. It is our unresolved wounds that are being resurrected in the present that cause distress. We must learn about our core issues, take care of ourselves properly, and communicate in responsible ways.

• •

5. **Use "And" as a conjunction instead of "But:"**

"I think what you said is important, *and* I have a different opinion."
Now feel the difference between these two sentiments:
"I love you *but*..."

"I love you *and*…"

What a difference the "and" makes! When you use "but" as a conjunction in most sentences, you annihilate all the good that you shared previous to the "but." After hearing "but," the listener will shut down and their walls will come up. Be sure to use "and" as a conjunction in all your personal and professional communications. This includes texting and emails.

"You're a great man, but your temper scares me."

"You're a great man, and your temper scares me."

6. Make a Reality Check:

If you think someone is thinking something about you or another person, then ask them if this is correct or not. For example, "Are you upset with me?" "Did you mean (such and such) when you said (such and such)?" Alfred Hitchcock's 1941 movie *Suspicion* is predicated upon a wife's fear that her husband is trying to kill her. Spoiler alert: Her hypothesis was found to be untrue at the end of the movie.

How many unnecessary arguments between spouses, friends, colleagues, and co-workers could be avoided if we only asked for clarification about what someone said, or what we thought they meant when they said something. I have experienced that our judgments are wrong at least 90% of the time. Please use a simple reality check to test your hypothesis. "Did you mean (such and such) when you said (such and such)?" If she tells you her truth then it is clear. If she decides to mask her real thoughts and feelings (that you judge she is really harboring in her mind and heart), you must leave it there. You cannot make anyone say or do what they are unwilling to say or do. The good news is, most people will share their truth with you.

Do not make assumptions. When I assume anything, I make an "ass" out of "u" and "me." Instead use a "reality check" if you think someone is upset with you. Here is an example of a reality check: "Were you angry with me when I saw you in the kitchen this morning?" A reality check is a litmus test about a belief or judgment that you have about another person. It helps objectify perceptions.

7. Remember - Expectations Kill:

Do not expect others to know what you need. It is important to learn to express your needs, rather than expect others to know what you want (expecting them to mind-read). Infants and toddlers expect us to know what they need because they are totally dependent upon the parent or caregiver for survival. As adults, we must learn to express that which we need rather than assume or expect others to know what we want, need, or desire.

8. Ask "How" and "What" questions, not "Why" questions:

"Why" questions send a person into her or his head, intellect. A "How" or "What" question helps her share more deeply, that which is in her heart. For example, "How was that like for you?" If you ask, "Why did you do that?" she immediately becomes more intellectual. "What did you go through?" "How did that make you feel?"

9. Recognize Triangulation:

If someone is upset with another person and shares with you about it, that is called triangulation. A is upset with B. Instead of A sharing directly with B about his grievance, he goes to C and shares about his consternation about B. Now C is triangulated between A & B, put in an impossible lose-lose situation. Here is a simple solution to this conundrum. When A shares with you about his being upset with B, simply say, "I know that you are upset with B,

I hear you, I understand. Honestly this issue is between the two of you. Please share directly with B about your thoughts, feelings, and needs. Thank you very much." Finished. It is not your job to save anyone else. It is not healthy or appropriate for you to be involved in their communication. Saviors not wanted!

10. Note that Men and Women Communicate Differently:

We all have different ways to express and receive love. Deborah Tannen, in her book *You Just Don't Understand*, says that men excel at "report talk" and women excel at "rapport talk." Generally speaking, men go straight to the point and want to fix things, while most women like to take their time describing their experiences and just need to be heard. Men, no fixing required!

One final simple yet profound point about personal communication:

We cannot give each other advice. When a wife tells her husband a very reasonable solution for a situation, she becomes his mother. "Sweetheart, I wish you would do the exercises in this TTT book. They will help you so much." When a husband does the same, gives simple advice to his wife, he becomes her father. Both do not receive the well-intentioned ideas no matter how brilliant or beautiful they may be. Of course, someone outside your couple can say the thing to your spouse and it's spot on! "Damn, I just told her the same thing!" Sorry, when you give advice to your partner, you become his or her parent. Off limits. Keep the peace. Be wise.

• •

Effective Listening and Sharing = Love.

• •

Dr. Harville Hendrix and his wife Dr. Helen LaKelly Hunt have developed a highly effective communication program called Safe

Conversations. Their goal is to help couples, families, communities, corporations, schools, and governments shift their culture from "competition between individuals" to a relational culture where "everyone collaborates." To find out more about their program: https://relationshipsfirst.org.

SECTION THREE—TALK

Family Healing

Temperament, Character, and Personality

It is essential to understand ourselves and each other. Who we are, a combination of inherited traits and acquired characteristics, impacts how we interact with our family, friends, and the world. Each of us has a basic temperament, character, and personality that make us who we are. By understanding these important distinctions, we may then understand the significant differences between ourselves, our loved ones, and our colleagues. Then we are able to use effective communication skills—listening, sharing, and negotiating—to achieve greater intimacy and love, rather than fighting and arguing because we do not understand our basic differences. Knowledge is power in all relationships.

> **Temperament**: innate traits, our biology
> **Character**: learned behaviors, environmental influences
> **Personality**: combination of our biology and learned behaviors

Temperament is the innate part of your personality that is inherited, it comes from your genes. "Because it's genetic and comes from your inherited traits, temperament is hard to modify, manipulate, or change. In some way or another, that tendency will always be there. But that doesn't mean you can't make an effort to encourage it or stop yourself from doing it."

Character: is the reflection of your experiences. "This is the aspect of personality that includes temperament (inherited traits) and the social and educational habits that you've learned … Character is the part of you that comes from your environment. It's also a result of the experiences and social interactions in your life, the ones you learn lessons from. And that makes it so these habits have an influence on your temperament and biological predispositions. The habits also adjust those predispositions and polish them, shaping your personality. That's why character's roots are in culture. It goes through different stages and takes its fullest form during adolescence. That's also why you can modify it and make changes to it."

Personality: is biology and learned behaviors. Personality is temperament (innate) and character (learned). "Personality is something that distinguishes individuals … according to many studies, it's stable over time and through different situations."

Retrieved from: https://exploringyourmind.com/the-differences-between-personality-temperament-and-character/ July 3, 2018

Four Temperaments

The Ancient Greek doctor Hippocrates came up with a theory of temperament based on the four humors or substances of yellow bile, black bile, phlegm, and blood. He believed that our personality and health depended on a balance of the four substances. Later Galen, a Greek physician, took Hippocrates theory and observed four types of people:

- **Choleric** (yellow bile): fire—passionate, energetic, easily angered, egocentric, extroverted, excitable, impulsive, task-oriented, ambitious, strong-willed, controlling, leadership skills, good planner, solution-oriented.
- **Melancholic** (black bile): earth—serious, introverted, cautious, suspicious, moody, focused, conscientious, do things alone.
- **Phlegmatic** (phlegm): water—private, thoughtful, calm, patient, caring, tolerant, rational, peaceful, steadfast, consistent, faithful.

- **Sanguine** (blood): air—happy, lively, sociable, talkative, optimistic, warm-hearted, artistic, flighty, changeable, make friends easily, struggles with fulfilling tasks.

Here you may access tests to determine your temperament:
https://psychologia.co/four-temperaments-test/
https://temperaments.fighunter.com/?page=test
https://four-temperaments.com

For further understanding, read Randy Rolfe's *The Four Temperaments* or from a Christian perspective read Tim LaHaye's *Spirit-Controlled Temperament*.

As you look at the four temperaments, did you determine yours and that of your partner? How about the temperaments of your children?

I have a choleric temperament, while my wife is certainly phlegmatic. I create, write, lead, teach, and counsel, while my wife is internal, private, caring, faithful, and supportive. Our three children cover the spectrum of sanguine, melancholic, phlegmatic, and choleric (or more specifically, each is a combination of the four temperaments—had to say that or I'd be in trouble with my kids!). Without understanding and appreciating each other's innate temperaments, we easily fight and argue. By respecting and appreciating each other's differences, we are able to express ourselves in a mature fashion—using effective listening and sharing skills—and then negotiate needs. What a difference it makes to understand ourselves and each other. Again, knowledge is power.

By comprehending your temperament and that of your loved ones and co-workers, you now have the ability to calm your mind by understanding that *you are created different, and differences are good*. By comprehending our temperamental differences, we expand our minds to embrace those unlike myself. Upon the foundation of this knowledge, we may learn to appreciate differences and thereby utilize a variety of communication skills to achieve greater intimacy in all relationships.

Personality paradigms

There are numerous personality archetypes developed by different psychologists. Here are just a few personality paradigms, in a vast sea of theories, to help you better understand yourself, your loved ones, and colleagues.

Myers Briggs

The Myers Briggs Type Indicator (MBTI) is a test to determine your personality. Many businesses have their employees take the Myer Briggs inventory so that each person may not only understand his or her personality style, but those of his or her colleagues. This leads to greater harmony and understanding between employers and employees. The same holds true for family members. Understanding the personality type of each family member also leads to greater understanding and peace. For more information check out: https://www.myersbriggs.org.

Myers-Briggs Type Indicator differentiates sixteen personality types (https://www.myersbriggs.org/my-mbti-personality-type/mbti-basics/the-16-mbti-types.htm):

1. **The Inspector (ISTJ):**
Quiet, serious, logical, orderly, practical, responsible, organized, value traditions and loyalty.

2. **The Nurturer (ISFJ)**
Quiet, friendly, responsible, conscientious, thorough, loyal, concerned with how others feel, strive to create an orderly and harmonious environment at work and at home.

3. The Counselor (INFJ)
Seek meaning and connection in ideas, relationships, and material possessions; organized, and decisive in implementing their vision.

4. The Mastermind (INTJ)
Often introverts, original ideas, implement their vision, achieve goals, see job through, skeptical, independent, high standards for themselves and others.

5. The Craftsman (ISTP)
Tolerant, flexible, quiet observers, act quickly, analyze what makes things work, interested in cause and effect, organize facts using logical principles, value efficiency.

6. The Composer (ISFP)
Quiet, friendly, sensitive, loyal, committed to their values and to people who are important to them. Dislike disagreements, do not force their opinions/values on others.

7. The Idealist (INFP)
Idealistic, loyal to values and to people; curious, quick to see possibilities, seek to understand people, help them fulfill their potential. Adaptable, flexible, and accepting.

8. The Thinker (INTP)
Seek to develop logical explanations, theoretical and abstract, interested more in ideas than in social interaction. Quiet, contained, flexible, and adaptable.

9. The Doer (ESTP)
Flexible, tolerant, pragmatic, focus on present, spontaneous, enjoy material comforts, learn by doing; act energetically to solve problems.

10. The Performer (ESFP)
Outgoing, friendly, accepting, flexible, exuberant lovers of life, people, and material things. Enjoy working with others to make things happen and make work fun.

11. The Champion (ENFP)

Warmly enthusiastic, imaginative, see life as full of possibilities; want a lot of affirmation from others, spontaneous and flexible, often rely on their ability to improvise.

12. The Visionary (ENTP)

Quick, ingenious, stimulating, alert, outspoken, resourceful in solving new and challenging problems, good at reading people, bored by routine.

13. The Supervisor (ESTJ)

Practical, realistic, decisive, quickly move to implement decisions. Organize projects and people to get things done, focus on getting results in the most efficient way possible.

14. The Provider (ESFJ)

Warmhearted, conscientious, cooperative, like harmony, efficient, loyal, follow through even in small matters. Notice what others need; want to be appreciated.

15. The Giver (ENFJ)

Warm, empathetic, responsive, responsible, loyal, highly attuned to the emotions, needs, and motivations of others. Find potential in everyone.

16. The Commander (ENTJ)

Decisive, assume leadership readily, quickly see illogical and inefficient procedures and policies, develop and implement comprehensive systems. Enjoy planning.

Excerpted from Introduction to Type® by Isabel Briggs Myers published by The Myers-Briggs Company. Used by permission.

SECTION THREE—TALK

"When you understand personality preferences, you can more readily appreciate differences between you and people closest to you, such as spouses, partners, children, and friends ... Knowledge of personality type allows you to see those differences as just those—different ways of 'being' ... Many couples learn to appreciate these differences and may even see them in a humorous light.

"Knowledge of type preferences can also help couples and families negotiate differences in several key approaches to lifestyle, intimacy, division of chores, managing money, and other areas of potential conflict."

Retrieved from: https://www.myersbriggs.org/type-use-for-everyday-life/psychological-type-and-relationships/

Enneagram Personality Types

The Enneagram Personality Types is another vehicle to understand oneself, one's partner, family members, friends, and colleagues.

"Everyone emerges from childhood with *one* of the nine types dominating their personality, with inborn temperament and other pre-natal factors being the main determinants of our type. This is one area where most all of the major Enneagram authors agree—*we are born with a dominant type*. Subsequently, this inborn orientation largely determines the ways in which we learn to adapt to our early childhood environment. It also seems to lead to certain unconscious orientations toward our parental figures, but why this is so, we still do not know."

The Riso-Hudson Enneagram Type Indicator (RHETI version 2.5) helps people identify their basic personality type.

Retrieved from: https://www.enneagraminstitute.com/how-the-enneagram-system-works

Nine Personality Types (https://www.enneagraminstitute.com):

1. **The Reformer**: Rational, Idealistic. Type: principled, purposeful, self-controlled, and perfectionistic.
2. **The Helper**: Caring, Interpersonal. Type: demonstrative, generous, people-pleasing, and possessive.
3. **The Achiever**: Success-Oriented, Pragmatic. Type: adaptive, excelling, driven, and image-conscious.
4. **The Individualist**: Sensitive, Withdrawn. Type: expressive, dramatic, self-absorbed, and temperamental.
5. **The Investigator:** Intense, Cerebral. Type: perceptive, innovative, secretive, and isolated.
6. **The Loyalist**: Committed, Security-Oriented. Type: engaging, responsible, anxious, and suspicious.
7. **The Enthusiast**: Busy, Fun-Loving. Type: spontaneous, versatile, distractible, and scattered.
8. **The Challenger**: Powerful, Dominating. Type: self-confident, decisive, willful, and confrontational.
9. **The Peacemaker**: Easygoing, Self-Effacing. Type: receptive, reassuring, agreeable, and complacent.

Let me say it once again: Knowledge is power and leads to greater understanding and more peaceful relationships.

Further reading:

1. *The Wisdom of the Enneagram: The Complete Guide to Psychological and Spiritual Growth for the Nine Personality Types,* by Don Richard Riso and Russ Hudson.
2. *Understanding the Enneagram: The Practical Guide to Personality Types,* by Don Richard Riso and Russ Hudson.
3. *The Enneagram: A Christian Perspective,* by Richard Rohr and Andreas Ebert.

Helen Fisher's Four Temperaments

Biological anthropologist Hellen Fisher describes four temperaments in her book *Why Him? Why Her?: Finding Real Love By Understanding Your Personality Type* (2009).

Here is a description of Dr. Fisher's four temperaments, including their dominant hormone:

Retrieved from: https://thoughtcatalog.com/january-nelson/2018/07/four-temperaments

Explorer (Dopamine) – Dominated by the pleasure neurotransmitter dopamine. Creative, curious, adventurous, impulsive, independent, risk-takers, high energy level and a profound need for novelty, excitement, and stimulation. Represent 26 percent of all people. Explorers are a good match for other Explorers—they need someone who is on the same level of energy and spontaneity.

Builder (Serotonin) – Dominated by serotonin, a neurotransmitter that is associated with sociability and serenity. Calm, cooperative, cautious, and consistent; make loyal friends and are quite attached to home and family. Represent 28.6 percent of the population. Low levels of anxiety and a high regard for tradition, pair best with their own type for romance. Marriages between two builders have a great chance of success.

Director (Testosterone) – Fueled by the male sex hormone testosterone, inventive, independent, assertive, competitive, decisive, and rational. Women as well as men can be dominated by testosterone. Represent 9.7 percent of females and 24.8 percent of men. Best love match with Negotiators.

Negotiator (Estrogen) – Intuitive, imaginative, idealistic, dominated by the female sex hormone estrogen. Introspective, big-picture thinkers who excel in verbal skills, consensus building, and long-term planning; shine when it comes to empathy, nurturing, and other social skills. Represent 20.4 percent of men and 35.8 percent of women. Best luck in love with Directors, whose decisiveness will complement their ambiguity.

Dr. Fisher describes why we are attracted to certain types.

"Men and women who were primarily novelty-seeking, energetic, curious and creative were statistically significantly more drawn to those who shared these traits, while those who were primarily conventional, cautious and rule following were also drawn to individuals like themselves. But those who were more analytical, tough minded, direct and decisive were disproportionately attracted to their opposite, those who were imaginative, intuitive, compassionate and socially skilled; and vice versa. In short, Explorers preferentially sought Explorers, Builders sought other Builders, and Directors and Negotiators were drawn to one another."

Retrieved from: http://www.helenfisher.com/downloads/articles/Article_%20We%20Have%20Chemistry.pdf

Take Helen Fisher's personality test: https://theanatomyoflove.com/relationship-quizzes/helen-fishers-personality-test/

Love Languages

Another paradigm explaining differences is the five love languages. One might say that love languages are tied to our temperament, an innate, biological trait inherited from birth. In his book *The Five Love Languages*, Gary Chapman states that each of us has a primary and secondary love language. Of course, it is best to experience all five. As you will now read, all five love languages are incorporated in TTT! Here is a brief summary of the five love languages.

Love Language 1: Words of Affirmation

1. Verbal compliments:
    a. Appreciate their being, who they are, i.e., their qualities and attributes. For example: "You are such a wonderful and masculine man. I appreciate your generous heart." "You are a very sensitive and gifted woman. You are beautiful and strong."
    b. Appreciate their behavior, what they do. For example: "You look sharp in that suit." "You look beautiful today." "I really appreciate your taking out the trash." "I admire your working so hard at school." "You're a wonderful provider for our family."
2. Words of encouragement: See the world through their eyes. Learn what is important to them. "Son, it's great you're in the school play. I know you'll do a wonderful job."
3. Words of affection: "I love you." "You mean so much to me." Tone is important.
4. Testify to others: speak affirming words about your partner or child in front of your family members and friends. Tell them how wonderful your partner or child is.
5. Written affirmations: Write affirming notes, letters, texts, or emails.

Love Language 2: Quality Time

1. Togetherness: Focus your undivided attention on your partner or child, and do what they like to do, not what you like to do.
2. Quality conversation: Use sympathetic dialogue and good listening skills, focused on what your partner or child is saying—their thoughts, feelings, and desires. Do not analyze or problem-solve, just use reflective listening skills.

3. Learn to share your thoughts, feelings, and desires without judging the other person. Use "I" statements, not "You" statements. If you have a different personality type—then it is important to establish regular sharing times to create balance in the relationship.
4. Quality activities: Provide wonderful memories that last a lifetime, i.e., camping, fishing, hiking, walks, attending a sporting event, play or concert, going on a trip together, family vacations. Participate in your partner or child's interests.

Love Language 3: Receiving Gifts

1. Gifts are meant to be an expression of love from the heart. They are visual symbols of love for the other person.
2. Find out what your partner or child likes. Investigate their desires and interests.
3. Gifts may be purchased or made. Spending money for your partner or child, whose love language is receiving gifts, will fill their love bucket.
4. Make rituals or ceremonies to place value on the giving of your gifts, whether for birthdays, anniversaries, holidays, special events, or just surprises. Gifts are an expression of your love, not just a material object.
5. Give the gift of yourself. Your physical presence is a powerful gift, especially in times of crisis or need.
6. Receiving gifts is unearned grace.
7. Note: Gifts should not be given out of guilt. That is counterfeit giving.

Love Language 4: Acts of Service

1. Do something special for your partner or child, i.e. build something together, teach them a skill, do homework

together, work on their car. This is an investment of time, effort, and heart.
2. Teach your partner or child to make requests, not demands. Do things they cannot do for themselves, or teach them something they do not know how to do but would like to learn. "Give a man a fish, and you feed him for a day. Teach him how to fish, and you feed him for a lifetime."
3. Ask your partner or child to make a list of things they would like you to do for them.

Love Language 5: Physical Touch

1. Physical touch communicates emotional love.
2. Babies must be held, kissed, rocked, cradled, and caressed in order to survive.
3. Adolescents and adults need lots of healthy touch in order to thrive.
4. Healthy non-sexual touch may consist of holding hands, hugging, putting your arm around their shoulder, and much more.
5. Touch = intimacy and love. Be flexible. Follow your partner or child's cues.

The love language of one family member is not necessarily the love language of the other. Ask questions to discover your partner and child's primary love language. "From your perspective, what would make our relationship better?" Observe their behavior and requests. These, too, will hold clues to their love languages. Experiment with the different love languages and see how they respond. Of course, our partner and children need and speak all five love languages. Give all five, and you will eventually discover their primary and secondary love languages. The chances are great that your love language and that of your partner and children are different.

Take the Five Love Language test: https://www.5lovelanguages.com

Identify the other person's love language, and then love them the way or ways in which they experience love. Practice, practice, practice. Dr. Greg Baer states, "Real love is caring about the happiness of another person without any thought for what we might get for ourselves" (*Real Love in Marriage*, New York: Gotham Books, 2006, page 4). Dr. Patricia Love states, "To be a true romantic, you have to see the world through your partner's eyes" (*Hot Monogamy*, 2012, page 181).

Birth Order

Austrian psychiatrist Alfred Adler was one of the first to suggest birth order influences personality development. He believed that birth order may leave an indelible impression upon our lives, impacting all intimate and work relationships.

Psychotherapist Sharon Wegsheider-Cruse adapted a birth order model from the work of Virginia Satir and other therapists. For more information about these family roles, please read *Another Chance: Hope and Health for the Alcoholic Family* by Sharon Wegsheider-Cruse. Here is a brief description of roles in an alcoholic or high stress, dysfunctional family system:

1. **Addict:** One parent may abuse substances (alcohol, drugs, medications, etc.) or is consistently angry (ragaholic). He uses substances, anger, sex, or controlling behaviors to numb his pain. He is emotionally detached from himself, his partner, and children.

2. **Enabler** (Caretaker): Stabilizing parent for the family system, trying desperately to reduce tension while simultaneously enabling their partner's substance abuse, anger, inappropriate sexual behaviors, or violence. This is quintessential codependency.

3. **Hero:** The first child receives all the attention of his parents and relatives. Oftentimes the oldest child will become the hero, trying to solve the parent's problems by over achieving academically and/or through extra-curricular activities. Of course, no matter how good she acts, the problems persist. As an adult, she may become a workaholic, prone to stress-related illnesses, and Type-A behaviors.

4. **Rebel/Scapegoat:** The second child witnesses the hero's behavior and reacts in a contrary manner, becoming a rebel with a cause. In reality, he is doing the same thing as the hero, trying desperately to receive love, attention, and affection from his parents, this time, through oppositional behavior. He becomes the scapegoat, blamed for the family problems. This child expresses the family's anger and frustration. He may become violent, and if the daughter is the rebel, she may be sexually promiscuous. Both are susceptible to drug abuse and hanging out with a gang.

5. **Lost child:** The third or youngest child may become a goody-goody, shy, withdrawn, and a loner. The parents are generally relieved that they don't have to contend with another rebellious child. The third or youngest child generally enjoys reading books, spending time in nature, and loves pets. As an adult, he or she may have difficulty with intimate relationships and may experience mental health issues.

6. **Mascot:** The fourth or youngest child acts like a performer, mascot, or clown, making everyone laugh and attempting to diffuse the tension in the family. He seeks the approval of others and is quite vulnerable. He doesn't understand why he feels so crazy, having internalized all the repressed feelings of the other family members. As an adult, he may be very anxious and need to use substances to self-medicate.

7. **The family pet** may also take on a role, acting as a source of affection, or become wild and weird. Our dog literally went insane due to the dysfunction of my family of origin. We eventually put her on a farm to recover!

8. **Only child**: The only child may take on multiple roles in the family, sometimes the hero, other times the rebel, loner, or mascot. It will depend upon her personality and family dynamics.

When the oldest child departs from home, the remaining children may shift roles. The importance of understanding these different positions is how they impact our adult lives and relationships. Unless we heal the wounds acquired in our family of origin, we will transport them into our new families. Healing is essential to break family curses. Please refer to all healing activities in the Time section.

Male / Female Differences

I would not dare to broach the vast subject about male and female differences. There are excellent books and YouTube videos that teach important lessons about how our brains, bodies, behaviors, and being are wired differently. My point in bringing this up is that it is essential for men and women to understand that we communicate with a different set of rules. Generally speaking, men share from their heads, while women listen with their hearts. *Men please take note*: It is important when communicating with your wife to make an emotional appeal. Trying to fix and intellectualize the problem will only lead to failure and an inability to connect with your female partner. If your wife is upset, just listen, paraphrase, or simply say, "Thank you (her name), tell me more." Please remember to be Mr. KYMS. Women, once again, you will need to bring your partner into the realm of reintegrating his emotions. Please teach him to speak from his heart. Use the Feelings Wheel regularly. Practice, practice, and practice.

A final skill for couples: Do not use the words "never" and "always" in your communications. When you use either of those two words, you are in fact regressing to your inner child. "You never do … with me." "You always do …" Those are the words of your inner child holding your partner hostage to past pain and unmet needs. Therefore, when communicating with your spouse, speak about a specific topic and do not globalize the subject.

Community Healing

It is easy to love those who are like ourselves. It is difficult to embrace those who have a different personality and hail from a different culture, religion, sexual orientation, or ethnicity. *Prejudice is an emotion.* It is illogical, stemming from a survival skill or a learned behavior from family and friends. Discrimination, the capacity to distinguish between my own kind and others, is actually a survival mechanism that was developed for our safety and well-being: to distinguish between my tribe, group, or safe environment, and to recognize potential threats and/or dangerous enemies. This, combined with the fight, flight, or freeze response, is for our safety and the survival of our loved ones. These evolutionary defenses—located in the amygdala, the limbic system of the brain where our emotions are stored—in a world of wounded and insecure people, become coping mechanisms and survival skills. These have nothing to do with logic. Therefore, shifting from disgust to compassion is not an easy journey, but very possible. Again, prejudice is learned or biological. Therefore, it will require conscious intention to unlearn and/or understand those different from me. Here is a simple formula to move from prejudice to compassion:

1. Allow yourself to feel disgust toward the other person (picture him in your mind). Do not try to fake compassion from the start. Tell yourself what you cannot stand about him. List, in your mind or write them down, the many reasons why you do not like him and what you find disgusting. Feel those feelings in your body. Where do you feel them? Identify the feelings and the locations in your body.

2. Now close your eyes and go inside. Ask yourself, "What is the origin of this feeling? Where did it come from?" Listen and wait for a response. This may take time as your heart and soul may

SECTION THREE—TALK

not trust you. The more you do inner child healing activities, the quicker your heart will share its truth. Once you discover the origin of the feeling, you may move to the next step. (You may need to repeat this process several times if there are multiple feelings with different locations in your body. Each may have a separate history and story to tell.)

3. "Does he represent someone in my past that hurt me?" Look into the eyes of the person that you do not like (of course, this is in your imagination). Now look behind him. Who, in your past, is like this person? Perhaps there are many others who carry similar energy or personalities. Just be quiet for a moment and look at these persons.

   Now it is your time to share how his behavior and/or his words made you feel. Let it out. Express your heart. Don't hold back. Take your time. Grieve, rage, release, and then breathe, take your power back, and ground yourself. Feel your heart and strength. You are loved, you are safe.*

4. Next, switch positions. Become the person who hurt you. Imagine what she or he felt, thought, and was going through at the time. Step into his shoes and speak as if you were he. Talk to yourself from his perspective. What does he want to say to you? What was he going through?

5. After he finishes sharing with you, step back into your position. Then look into his eyes. How do you feel now? Can you see his brokenness? Can you better understand his wounds and situation? By standing in another person's shoes, you begin to transform enmity to understanding.

6. You may need to repeat this process several times, and perhaps with different figures from your past that betrayed, hurt, or abused you.

* In step three, when you are expressing your feelings, you may need to ground yourself after this process. There is a concept in Neuro-Linguistic Programming (NLP) and Hypnosis called an "anchor." An anchor is a stimulus that is associated with a particular state of mind or mood. An anchor may be a memory of love from your past. Whenever you are sad, mad, or afraid, call to mind this beautiful memory of love. This represents your anchor to become more centered, grounded, and peaceful. At this moment as you read these words, call to mind a beautiful memory of love. Close your eyes to see and sense it. Then as you picture this scene, touch a place on your body, perhaps put your hand on your chest, or your hand on your elbow or knee. Associate this memory of love when touching the particular part of your body. This will now become your anchor in times of need.

It may be necessary to have a therapist, trusted loved one or friend guide you through this exercise. By going through this process of bleeding your personal wounds, you will eventually begin to see the "other" as myself. We are all hurting, wounded, and in need of love. Remember, there is only love or lack of love (which we often call "evil").

Additionally, you may dislike another person because he or she represents:

a. Your disowned parts: parts of your personality that you never developed as a child. If you are generally quiet and shy, you may dislike the talkative or loud person. Deep within your psyche is perhaps an angry and/or jealous inner child, "I wish that I had a voice!"

b. Lost parts: parts of your personality that you had to bury or repress as a child in order to survive. You became the caretaker of others at your own expense. Therefore, you may dislike those who know how to take care of themselves, taking time to live out their passions. Perhaps you lost that part of your personality.

c. Perpetrators: those who hurt you as a child. This "type" of person may continue to manifest himself in your life, over and over again. "Why am I attracted to people who hurt me?" We magnetically attract those who represent our perpetrators, because our inner child is always trying to obtain lost love. Until we resolve those wounds, and experience healthy self-love and the love of others, we will continue to resurrect our past in present-day relationships.

d. Learned prejudice: family, friends, and community may have taught you to dislike different types of people, races, religions, etc. "Jews are all the same, greedy, selfish people." "Muslims are all terrorists." "Italians are all in the mafia." Notice the word "all" in these stereotypical descriptions. This type of prejudice is learned behavior from environmental influences.

e. Innate prejudice: we fear those we do not understand, and behaviors that differ from ours. If you have heterosexual desires, when seeing two men kiss your stomach may turn. "That's disgusting," is the internal voice. Why? Because of the biological, preservation instinct that is a built-in defense mechanism to protect ourselves and our loved ones. Only by listening to, and learning about those who are different from you, will your natural biological prejudice begin to wane and compassion ensue.

When you do not forgive those who hurt you as a child, you are forever attached to them, like two links of a chain. When you forgive, you break the chain that bound you together. Actually forgiveness is a gift you give yourself. In this way you let go of the other and become free.

When you argue or fight with another person, it is always about you and not about them (remember, when you point your index finger at the other person, three fingers are pointing back at you!). Your inner child is empty, afraid, wounded, and/or reacting (fight, flight, or freeze response). Ask for a "time out," and calm yourself down to figure out what triggered you in the first place. All conflicts in the present are re-enactments of unresolved issues from your past, or represent present-day issues, i.e., exhaustion, conflict at work, fear of financial issues, etc. You may use the above protocol to figure out what is triggering you in the moment.

Own your issues. Blaming others is always a lose-lose situation. You give your personal power away to the other person when you blame her or him. Then you are a victim living in Victimland, speaking Victimese! TTT is calling forth all Victors of Love. Reclaim your personal power by experiencing self-love and giving the gift of love to others. Remember the great commission from Deuteronomy 6:5 and Leviticus 19:18: "Love the Lord your God with all your heart, with all your soul, and all your might. And love your neighbor as yourself." The implication and order of love is to: 1) experience God's love, 2) love God, 3) love yourself, and 4) love others. If you do not experience being loved, and learn to love yourself, self-hatred works its way outward (just as self-love does).

Honor differences:

   a. Opinions
   b. Facts
   c. Values
   d. Personality Styles
   e. Gender roles: Martians, Venetians
   f. Races: black, white, yellow, red, pink, purple, and all mixed up (the ideal)
   g. Cultural heritage: European, Latino, Asian, Middle-Eastern, American, etc.

h. Religious traditions: Catholic, Christian, Jewish, Islam, Hindu, etc.

i. Sexual orientations: heterosexual, homosexual, and in between

Most of us are not honest with each other because we fear being rejected or hurting someone's feelings. You are not that powerful! You are not responsible for someone's feelings (unless you are God, and then we will all follow you!). You are responsible TO others: to be genuine, honest, and loving. The only ones that you are responsible FOR are your children when they are growing up in your home. When they become adults, you no longer are responsible FOR them, but TO them. Stop playing the "God" card and be yourself. If people like you, great. If they don't, great.

• •

*Life is a come as you are party,
not a popularity contest!*

• •

Nelson Mandela referenced the wonderful quote by Marianne Williamson:

"Our deepest fear is not that we are inadequate. Our deepest fear is that we are powerful beyond measure. It is our light, not our darkness that most frightens us. We ask ourselves, Who am I to be brilliant, gorgeous, talented, fabulous? Actually, who are you *not* to be? You are a child of God. Your playing small does not serve the world. There is nothing enlightened about shrinking so that other people won't feel insecure around you. We are all meant to shine, as children do. We were born to make manifest the glory of God that is within us. It's not just in some of us; it's in everyone. And as we let our own light shine, we unconsciously give other people permission to do the same. As we are liberated from our own fear, our presence automatically liberates others" (*A Return to Love*, New York: Harper Collins, 1992, pages 190-191).

Building community means getting to know people unlike yourself. Reach out across the divide of differences. Listen, learn, and ultimately love those who are different from you, and may teach you, and thereby enrich your life as you enrich theirs. Move from disgust to compassion and love. Bless and be blessed.

Conclusion: Final Touch!

Beauty and the Beast was originally written by French novelist Gabrielle-Suzanne Barbot de Villeneuve in 1740. Belle, the female protagonist of the story, wins the heart of the Beast with higher love. She agrees to pay her father's debt by living in the castle of the Beast. When she disobeys his order, not to go into the West Wing, she apologizes. He becomes enraged, and she states that she will not stand for his inappropriate behavior. She flees the castle and is surrounded by a pack of wolves. The Beast comes to her aide and saves her life. Upon their return to the castle she thanks him, and he says, "This wouldn't have happened if you didn't run away." To which she replies, "I wouldn't have run away if you didn't treat me the way you did." Then he remains silent as she was indeed correct about his inappropriate behavior.

Belle is one of the most evolved characters of any story or movie. She has internalized her parent's love, has a healthy sense of self-worth, a well-rounded personality, enjoys reading and learning about foreign lands and other people, and finally, she is full of compassion and love for others. Having a strong ego-structure, she would not let anyone treat her inappropriately, even in the face of adversity. Let us all aspire to emulate this wonderful example of compassion, an evolved higher self, curiosity of those different from ourselves, and emboldened with greater love.

TIME represents sunlight. Time to get in touch with your soul, heal your wounds, and fulfill your unmet love needs. No one will love or respect you if you don't love or respect yourself. World peace begins within. Self-hatred works its way outward, affecting all of our personal and professional relationships. Hurting people hurt people. In the same way, self-love extends outward. In the TIME section, you learned skills for proper self-care, and how to encourage the health and healing of your family and community. Healing people heal people.

TOUCH is like water for all relationships. Without water we die. Touch is the most important and the most neglected of our five senses. Because there is great confusion between sex, love, and intimacy, we have been denied the natural benefits of healthy touch in our daily lives. We are born with skin hunger as infants. If those primal needs went unmet in early childhood, if we were misused, abused, or neglected, we may spend the rest of our lives looking for love in unhealthy relationships or behaviors—porn and masturbation for men, romance novels and erotica for women, and hooking up with multiple sex partners. We must learn how to give and receive healthy touch *on a daily basis* with family, friends, faith community, and co-workers. We must reclaim our right to healthy touch in our families and community. In the TOUCH section you learned skills to bring hope and healing into your lives, and the lives of your loved ones and community.

TALK, or good communication, is the Air for all personal and professional relationships, which includes both listening and sharing. We need to learn the art of effectively sharing our thoughts, feelings, and needs. Equally important is to learn the art of listening, which takes twice as much energy as it does to share. Remember, we have two ears and one mouth, so we need to listen twice as much as we speak. In the Talk section you learned about effective listening and sharing skills, different personality styles, love languages, gender differences, birth order, and cultural backgrounds.

Now is the time to **Actionize** all the skills that you have learned throughout this book. *Without action nothing changes.* The road to hell is paved with good intentions. *Succeed small rather than fail big.* Choose one skill or exercise from any of the three sections and start using it today. Make a list of your goals and a specific schedule to complete each task. For example, "I will begin to do all the exercises in *Recovery of Your Inner Child*, one chapter every two weeks. By such-and-such a date I will complete all these exercises. Then I will make an Affirmation MP3 recording. I will first make my lists, then find friends and mentors to do the recordings, put beautiful music in the background, and then begin to listen daily on such-and-such a date. After that, I will start to do all the exercises in *Ten Days to Self-Esteem*. I will begin on such-and-such a date, doing one chapter every two weeks, and finish by such-and-such a date." On our website we have both inner child and affirmation meditations to supplement inner child and self-esteem work.

Make a concrete treatment plan for healing that involves Time, Touch & Talk exercises. For proper self-care, it is imperative to create a strong support system. This may take time to develop. Look for local and/or online support groups. Whatever issue or issues you are dealing with, there are groups created to help you. Just do an online search and you will find local or virtual groups. Please be mindful to find a group that fits your spiritual needs. There are many faith-based support groups. The recovery movement is excellent, and yet, for those who uphold traditional Biblical principles, you will need to search for like-minded groups.

A study published in the journal PLOS ONE, October 2018 speaks about the benefits of hugging: *Receiving a hug is associated with the attenuation of negative mood that occurs on days with interpersonal conflict*, authored by Michael L. Murphy, Denise Janicki-Deverts, and Sheldon Cohen. "Interpersonal touch is emerging as an important topic in the study of adult relationships, with recent research showing that such behaviors can promote better relationship functioning and individual wellbeing." (Retrieved from: https://journals.plos.org/plosone/article?id=10.1371/journal.pone.0203522.)

• •

Many people in our culture and world today are oversexed because they are undernourished, lacking healthy, non-sexual touch on a regular basis. Porn and erotica provide a way to objectify people without ever really touching them.

• •

Many sincere devotees of Christianity, Catholicism, Judaism, Islam, Hinduism, and other faiths believe one thing about sex—that it should be reserved as a sacred covenant between one man and one woman in marriage—and yet practice an entirely different ethos. I know for a fact that some pastors believe that Jesus did not talk specifics when it comes to sex, except adultery and divorce. They reference other Biblical passages, i.e. Old Testament standards about multiple wives and partners, as a way to permit them to stray outside of the marriage covenant to satisfy needs which go unmet in their marital relationships. Others believe that it is OK to stray, just ask God for forgiveness and He will wipe your slate clean. What about single and divorced men and women, and widows? And what about LGBT persons who believe that homosexual behavior is incompatible with their spiritual beliefs? Don't these single, divorced, widowed, and LGBT persons have the right to fulfill their sexual needs? Not an easy question to answer. I believe that this conundrum is similar in all faiths. Some pastors, priests, rabbis, imams, and other religious leaders preach and teach one thing, yet practice another. And so it trickles down to their flocks, and in most houses of worship worldwide, there is an unspoken rule—we believe one thing, and practice another. In the words of my mother, "Do as I say, not as I do!"

The revolutionary concept of TTT, as a way to fulfill deeper needs for love and intimacy without sex, is not in the realm of belief in the minds and hearts of many religious leaders. They are stuck in a lose-lose system revolving around prohibitions, seeking justification or permission to wander, rather than solutions for their primal needs for connection, bonding, and intimacy with another human being, *sans the sex*. We all need to be held, heard, and healed. We all need to be validated just for who we are. We all need to be celebrated as a magnificent son or daughter of God. TTT is a celebration of life, love, and the art of achieving true intimacy between two people that need not include sex.

Making love is beautiful. Making love is fun. Making love is the highest art form of true intimacy and vulnerability between a husband and wife. True love-making takes time to develop. Real love-making, knowing the needs of my partner, pleasing her the way she wants to be pleased, and she in turn learning how to please her man; mutually satisfying each other's needs, all the while exploring new ways to enjoy each other ... well that's a lifetime pursuit of joy and real intimacy.

TTT will help you fill the hole in your soul: the soul being your heart, mind, and will. Many are so empty, so very empty. Many who are in responsible positions both in personal relationships and/or leadership positions, are very empty and hungry for love. They have so many unmet needs, so they do that which they don't want to do. They need love and often settle for sex (virtual or real), either within or outside of the marriage bed. However sex does not heal deeper needs because it is the soul crying out for love. Sex will not heal our wounds or help meet our deeper needs, because the need is that of a child within, or an adult who is exhausted and needs to receive affection—be heard, held, and loved. By getting your needs met through healthy touch, by being heard and honored for who you are, then you won't have to feel guilt and shame because you don't have to do that which you don't want to do. And now allow me to introduce Phase Two of the TTT project:

A Dream for the Future: TTT Centers

Our plan is to create TTT centers throughout the world. In the TTT center you may request to be held by a man or woman, by someone young, or an elder, for 15 minutes, 30 minutes, 45 minutes, one hour or more. Beautiful men and women in private TTT rooms will hold you, honor you, and cherish you. It will be a safe place to be held, heard, and healed, all in complete safety with confidentiality. And, no sex necessary, required, or offered!

In our TTT centers you will find healthy sources of love and affection to fill the void in your soul, the tiredness and exhaustion from giving and giving, and always being the responsible person. TTT is a safe place where you may get your needs met and feel loved just for who you are, not for what you do, not for how you look, but just for who you are. Please continue to check out our website for more details about the creation of TTT centers near you: www.TimeTouchandTalk.com.

We will eventually create a TTT app. Instead of using the Tindr or Grindr apps to hook-up with people, you may find a wonderful, safe, and nourishing experience at our TTT center, sans the sex. If you are interested in becoming part of our TTT movement, please contact us. We are especially looking for men and women who are trained therapists/counselors/coaches, and anyone with professional training in the healing arts of healthy touch. Email us at: TTT@TimeTouchandTalk.com.

Time, Touch & Talk is the beginning of a new global paradigm shift to create a world culture of true intimacy. Touching not only our pets, but one another. We will learn to hug and hold each other in safety.

There is a Catch 22 phenomenon in the religious community: Don't Look, Don't Touch, and Don't Tell. This creates more need, more danger, increased chemical arousal, more frustration, and the desire to act out inappropriately. Instead of fostering prohibitions, let us promote solutions—healthy touch in all avenues of life. Present this book to your spiritual leader and suggest the commencement of a healthy touch program in your place of worship. In the Catholic Church, part of the service, or Mass, is greeting one another by saying, "Peace be with you."

It would be natural to add a hug when speaking this simple phrase. Many Christian churches also make time in their services for greeting guests and fellow members. Incorporating hugs would also be natural during this portion of the service. The church, synagogue, or mosque should be the safest place on earth to give and receive healthy touch. I am fully aware that in various countries and religious traditions touching another person is taboo, therefore we will have to work within the construct of their traditions. And yet, we may slowly introduce incremental changes to help heal humanity through the power of healthy touch.

Nothing is more powerful than an idea whose time has come. It is time to lay down the weapons of war and reach out with our arms. No more arms of war, but arms of affection. They are the greatest weapons of all—to touch and to be touched. That is our challenge. Teaching healthy touch to our children, so that they may cross cultural, religious, racial, gender, and sexual/gender orientation divides, creating a new world order. High tech, high touch, lots of love.

Rather than focusing on one scandal after another, let us focus on preventing them in the first place by implementing Touch Programs. First and foremost, begin a Touch Program in your family. *Succeed small rather than fail big.* Introduce one simple new touch activity. Let your kids know that every morning and evening you will give them a 60-second hug, or start with a 10-second hug. You may increase the length of hugging time as you all become more comfortable.

Practice this for several months. Next introduce looking into each other's eyes and sharing your thoughts, feelings, and needs. Use the Feelings Wheel. Take your time. *Succeed small rather than fail big.* Then introduce placing your arm around your son or daughter's shoulders, walking hand-in-hand down the street. What? In this country? Yes, in every country of the world. This is the norm in the Middle East and several Asian countries. Let us inherit this tradition and restore the devastation of the Puritanical traditions that sickly sexualized our society.

Then extend this Touch Program to include your friends. Next, carry this into your community: groups, places of worship, and with co-workers. The sooner you get started, the sooner you will reap the benefits of healthy touch. Your life will significantly improve both personally and professionally.

We do not need to be at our best only when crises occur. We can do it every day of our lives. Women, start teaching your men how to touch, how to hug, how to hold, how to cuddle without having sex. Stop the unhealthy repetition of history in families: men do not meet their wife's needs, so the wife leans on her son(s) to get her emotional needs met. Then when he grows up he doesn't know how to take care of his wife, treating her the same way that his dad treated his mom (Monkey See, Monkey Do, repeating his father's sad behavior), then his wife uses her son(s) to get her emotional needs met, and on it goes throughout generations ... until someone takes responsibility. Start a Touch Program in your family today. TTT is the way to heal the world through healthy touch.

• •

Our greatest natural resource is our arms, human arms, to hold another man, woman, or child. That is our greatest resource, a secret weapon! Sex has been a substitute for love far too long. It has not worked yet, and it will never will. Healing the world through healthy touch is the new world order.

• •

TTT is all about spending Time together, Touching in healthy ways, and Talking responsibly, sharing, and listening, and meeting needs. Angry boys with big guns are hurt souls. Hurting people hurt people. The Eminems of the world need us. When you see Eminem, give him a big hug and kiss for me. Oh yes, many kisses too! Not sexual, mind you, just good, healthy, safe kisses on the cheek. Just pretend you live in Europe, the Middle East, Latin America, or hail from a Jewish family! Healthy hugs and kisses are going to be the salve that soothes hurting children and adults. *Healing people heal people.*

TTT = Timeless Treasures of the Heart. Would you please write a song, poem, or make a video about TTT and post it on our TTT YouTube Channel? Link? Let's rock the world with TTT!

In Maya Angelou's book, *I Know Why the Caged Bird Sings*, she writes about her experience of childhood sexual abuse and rape at eight years old, then remaining mute for the next five years. "We don't choose the things we believe in; they choose us," (*Minority Report*, movie). Our gift is through the wound. God made me a very kinesthetic man. Then I was sexually abused. My father did not experience being held as a child as he grew up in military school. He was touch deprived his entire childhood, and therefore unable to touch and hold me. My mother held me too close, and I experienced her pain and frustrations.

CONCLUSION: FINAL TOUCH!

As you've seen in the previous pages, I was introduced to sex by my Uncle Pete at five, and then by friends in middle and high school. I then spent years looking for love in all the wrong places, and in all the wrong ways. With the help of Phillip, Peter, Russell, Jae Sook, Victoria, and Hilde, the walls around my heart began to melt and the love came in to the deepest core of my being. Without their loving arms around my fractured body and soul, I would have died. Then Jarish, Jessica, and Alfred would never have been born; our three extraordinary children, now fulfilling their remarkable destinies.

I have learned the hard way about the healing powers of healthy Time, Touch & Talk. Please join me in helping the world heal a little more through TTT. I am the King of Touch. You can be the King and Queen of Touch too! This is a Battle of Love for our children, and for our world. Who will win?

• •

She or he who loves the most and the longest will be the Victors of Love.

• •

The #MeToo and #TimesUp Movements are making waves to stop the abuse of power. Now the TTT Movement will provide solutions, creating a world of intimacy without having to misuse sex. Artificial Intelligence will never come close to providing the warmth of loving arms around you. Pass it on. Actions speak louder than words. Let's get in touch with ourselves and each other. Pass on the gift of healthy touch. Visit one of our TTT centers and receive healthy touch today, where you will be held, heard, and healed.

Children and adults with Down's Syndrome hug everyone. We think it is great. Now it is our time to do the same. If you are inspired by these ideas, and you want to be involved in this new paradigm, please help us create TTT centers in your community. Contact our office at: TTT@TimeTouchandTalk.com.

Brene Brown, Ph.D., a research professor at the University of Houston, has authored nine books, the latest being *Dare to Lead*. Her TED talk on The Power of Vulnerability has already received over 37 million views. Her research is about vulnerability, courage, authenticity, and shame. I mention Dr. Brown's work as an example of creating a new world order of connection, belonging, and intimacy.

• •

The hand that rocks the cradle rules the world.
—*J. Edgar Hoover.*

• •

There are many different types of wounds that healthy touch will heal:

1. Hetero-emotional wounds between father and daughter, and mother and son.
2. Homo-emotional wounds between father and son, and mother and daughter.
3. Additionally: sibling wounds, sexual abuse wounds, physical abuse wounds, neglect, and more:
    - Male mentors will help women resolve and heal their father wounds and fulfill legitimate unmet love needs.
    - Male mentors will help men resolve and heal their father wounds and fulfill legitimate unmet love needs.
    - Female mentors will help men resolve and heal their mother wounds and fulfill legitimate unmet love needs.
    - Female mentors will help women resolve and heal their mother wounds and fulfill legitimate unmet love needs.

TTT centers will have both male and female mentors to help you restore lost love and heal unresolved wounds. TTT centers will eventually extend to college campuses, work campuses, office buildings, hotels, and spas.

• •
We are here to make your dreams come true.
We offer everything but sex!
• •

In all my life, I never imagined that God would use me, a Jewish, Christian, Catholic man to bring understanding and healing to the world through healthy Time, Touch & Talk. My life has been completely unconventional from start to finish. This book and the TTT project has been a dream for 22 years. In the past three years while writing this book, I had to pass through hell over and over again to rediscover the meaning of these principles.

There was a great price to pay to uncover the truth about healthy Time, Touch & Talk. I lovingly and freely bestow these gifts upon you. Additionally, I am fully aware that the exercises and concepts contained in this TTT book are just the beginning. Please use the suggested references at the back of the book to deepen your understanding and personal healing. And once again: *Actionize all that you have learned.* Succeed small rather than fail big.

Please remember always and forever that Touch ≠ Sex. By fulfilling skin hunger in healthy, non-sexual ways, we will ↑ Productivity, ↑ Well Being, ↑ Self-Worth, ↑ Happiness, and ↑ Compassion.

TTT+

For those in leadership positions who are hurting and in desperate need of assistance, we offer an additional service called TTT+. If you are burned out, over-worked, have been taking care of your family and business/ministry/public service, and just can't take another day; if you have been in ministry/public service for years and years and don't have one more day left in you; if you have been doing that which you don't want to do, and want to stop; if you have reached the height of your dreams, accomplished more than imagined, given your heart and soul to so many, and can't go on one more day; if you are aching inside, have given your best for so many, and you just need someone or some people to honor you, to hold you, to comfort you, to love you, to just be there for you … TTT+ is here to fulfill your needs.

We have created a team of seasoned and loving souls to fulfill your deepest needs so that you may fall apart in our arms. It's your time to be loved, to be held, to be heard, to be healed … to be honored for all the years of sacrifice and service, and so much more. Our TTT+ team is waiting for you.

You don't need to keep doing things you don't want to do for even one more day! It's time for you to receive in healthy ways, and we will create a ceremony to honor your heart, mind, body, and spirit—the whole of you will be held and heard and taken such great care of, like you've never been loved before. TTT+ was created just for you. It's Time, Touch & Talk+ to heal the weary, wounded, and wandering soul. We Are Here For You. Call our office to discuss your needs. We guarantee the strictest of confidentiality. Your needs will be held sacred and safe.

For the rest of us, I hope to see you at one of our TTT centers. Until then, actionize these principles, change yourself, and the world will change with you!

References for Further Healing

Embracing Ourselves, Hal and Sidra Strone, Ph.D., (Voice Dialogue), New World Library, 1998.

Focusing, Eugene Gendlin, Ph.D., Bantam Books, New York, 1982.

Healing the Child Within, by Dr. Charles L. Whitfield, M.D., Health Communications, 1987.

The Healing Power of Humor, Allen Klein, Jeremy P. Tarcher, Inc, Los Angeles, CA, 1989.

Holding Time, Martha Welch, M.D., Fireside Book, Simon & Schuster, New York, 1988.

Mindful Loving: 10 Practices for Creating Deeper Connections, Henry Grayson, Ph.D., 2003, Penguin Publishing Group, New York.

Recovery of Your Inner Child, Lucia Capacchione, Ph.D., Simon & Schuster, Fireside Book, New York, 1991.

Self-Parenting: The Complete Guide to Your Inner Conversations, by John K. Pollard III, Generic Human Studies Publishing, Rancho Cordova, CA, 2018.

What you Feel You Can Heal, John Gray, Ph.D., Heart Publishing, Mill Valley, CA, 1993.

Raising An Emotionally Intelligent Child: The Heart of Parenting, John Gottman, Simon & Schuster, New York, 1998.

Real Love and *Real Love in Marriage*, Greg Baer, Avery publishing, 2004 & 2007.

Self-Sabotage, Martha Baldwin, Grand Central Publishing, 1990.

The Secret Life of the Unborn Child, Thomas Verny, M.D., with John Kelly, Dell Publishing, New York, 1981.

Ten Days to Self-Esteem, David Burns, Harper Collins, New York City, New Your, 1993.

Touch Therapy, Helen Colton, Kensington Publishing Corp., New York, 1983.

Touching: The Human Significance of Skin, Ashley Montague, Ph.D., Harper & Row Publishers, New York, 1986.

You Just Don't Understand: Women and Men in Conversation, Deborah Tannen, Ballantine Books, New York, 1990.

Why Marriages Succeed or Fail...And How You Can Make Your Last, John Gottman, Fireside Book, Simon & Schuster, New York, 1994.

Family Healing Sessions

The Family Healing Session (FHS) is one of the most advanced and effective therapeutic tools available in family counseling. The FHS helps generate greater intimacy and loving relationships within the family. It is especially helpful to remove barriers that prevent healthy connection and communication between parents and children. It also supports the resolution of longstanding conflicts in the family.

Ideally the parents and all the children participate in the FHS. It has been said by many—who have participated in our Family Healing Sessions—that this experience was equal to and greater than several years of therapy!

Resolving Conflicts through Parent-Child Bonding

The purpose of the Family Healing Session is to connect the wounded adult-child (or children) to his or her parents and/or siblings. The child's struggle then becomes an opportunity for the entire family to come together and heal.

Through any hurtful incident that a child experienced in the past, separation might have occurred in the parent-child relationship. If a trauma or emotional detachment goes unrecognized and unresolved, the wounding within the child will result in the development of a "symptom" in order to cope with the underlying pain. Through our Family Healing Sessions, the parents and children express their pent-up emotions and wounds. As a result of this process, they experience beautiful bonding and renewed love!

Finally the child will feel safe, secure, and experience the magnificent sensation, "I belong."

Summary of what you will receive:

- Family Healing Session for parents and children: Two-day intensive
- Personal Treatment Plan: How to continue parent-child bonding
- Aftercare program, ongoing support

Please email us at: TTT@TimeTouchandTalk.com if you would like more information about a Family Healing Session or Tel. (301) 805-5155.

About the Author

Richard Cohen, M.A., is a psychotherapist, educator, and author who travels throughout the United States, Europe, Latin America, and the Middle East teaching about marital relations, communication skills, parenting skills, healing from sexual abuse, and understanding gender identity and sexual orientation issues. Over the past 30 years, he has helped hundreds in therapy and thousands through healing seminars, as well as trained over 6,000 physicians, psychologists, counselors, and ministry leaders how to assist those dealing with gender identity and sexual orientation concerns. Cohen is the author of 1) *Being Gay: Nature, Nurture, or Both?*, 2) *Gay Children Straight Parents: A Plan for Family Healing*, 3) *Loving Our Gay Family Members, Friends, and Neighbors*, 4) *Healing Humanity: Time, Touch & Talk*, and soon-to-be released, 5) *TTT Parenting*. He also authored a ground-breaking Counselor Training Program: Assisting Those with Same-Sex Attraction and Their Loved Ones which is available as a 16-disc CD series, MP3 download, and 180-page manual.

He founded the International Healing Foundation (IHF) in 1990, and is currently the president and co-founder of Positive Approaches To Healthy Sexuality (PATH). Based in the Washington, D.C. metropolitan area, PATH offers counselor training programs, family healing session, consultations, resource materials, and speaking engagements. Cohen is a frequent guest lecturer on college and university campuses, and at therapeutic and religious conferences.

Cohen holds a Bachelor's degree from Boston University and a Master's of Arts degree in counseling psychology from Antioch University. He has worked in child abuse treatment services, and individual, couples, and family therapy services. For three years, he worked as an HIV/AIDS educator for the Seattle, Washington chapter of the American Red Cross where he authored a statewide curriculum for foster parents and health care providers dealing with HIV infected children.

Cohen has been interviewed by newspaper, radio and television media including appearances on 20/20, Jimmy Kimmel Live, Larry King Live, The O'Reilly Factor, CNN, and other news outlets throughout the world. He lives in the Washington, D.C., metropolitan area with his wife of thirty-nine years, while his three adult children are making their mark in the world.

Time, Touch & Talk
P.O. Box 2315, Bowie, MD 20718
Tel. (301) 805-5155 / Fax (301) 805-0182

Email: TTT@TimeTouchandTalk.com
www.TimeTouchandTalk.com

Writing the outline for the TTT book at Montserrat Monastery near Barcelona, Spain, during the month of February 2018. While writing the book, I listened to recordings of the Montserrat Boys Choir for over one year.

www.ingramcontent.com/pod-product-compliance
Lightning Source LLC
LaVergne TN
LVHW021654060526
838200LV00050B/2349